D   ics

DELIBERATIVE GLOBAL POLITICS

Discourse and Democracy in a Divided World

John S. Dryzek

polity

First published in 2006 by Polity Press
Reprinted 2008

Polity Press
65 Bridge Street
Cambridge CB2 1UR, UK

Polity Press
350 Main Street
Malden, MA 02148, USA

ISBN–10: 0–7456–3412–5
ISBN–13: 978–07456–3412–8
ISBN–10: 0–7456–3413–3 (pb)
ISBN–13: 978–07456–3413–5 (pb)

A catalogue record for this book is available from the British Library.

Typeset in 11 on 13 pt Berling
by Carnegie Publishing Ltd, Lancaster.

Printed and bound in Great Britain by MPG Books Ltd, Bodmin, Cornwall

For further information on Polity, visit our website: www.polity.co.uk

Contents

Preface

Many if not most of the main axes of conflict in today's world can be interpreted in terms of contending discourses. Discourses are sets of concepts, categories, and ideas that provide ways to understand and act in the world, whether or not those who subscribe to them are aware of their existence. Their role is not universally appreciated, especially by those wedded to more traditional interpretations of international politics that see conflict as being generated by differences across material entities such as states, alliances, corporations, social movements, or terrorist networks. Those who do appreciate the role of discourses often treat them as singular and accepted, rather than multiple and contested. While discourses have always been important in ordering the system, what is different about the evolving world is the degree to which discourses are amenable to contestation. At one level this is bad news: for the resultant conflict can be violent. At another level this contestation is good news: for it opens the door to decentralized, reflective, and so democratic control over the engagement of discourses. This possibility holds even when it comes to the most murderous sorts of conflict across identities that can only be validated by violent opposition to the identity of the other side.

This book therefore has two facets. One is explanatory, an accounting of the world's conflicts in terms of clashing discourses. The other is normative, outlining the project of a transnational discursive democracy that could constitute the essence of deliberative global politics.

There are two kinds of deliberative global politics. The first would look to deliberation in the context of international negotiations between states and others, and within international governmental organizations such as the European Union, United Nations, and World Trade Organization. The second would emphasize deliberation in the context of diffuse engagement of discourses in international public spheres concerned with public affairs, but not seeking to exercise formal policy-making authority. While accepting that both are important, I emphasize the second. The reason is that deliberation closely tied to the construction and application of formal authority in the international system is not easily rendered democratic, as it normally takes place among executives or their nominees (be they from states, corporations, or international organizations). Democratic legitimacy enters only tenuously, to the degree these executives are themselves elected by or responsible to some body of citizens, somewhere. Thus deliberative *and democratic* global politics may most fruitfully be sought in the more informal realm of international public spheres and the engagement of discourses that they can feature. This emphasis enables connections to be made to recent developments in democratic theory.

The project of transnational discursive democracy that I sketch is not the only democratization project currently alive in international politics. In the concluding chapter I return to a comparison with two other prominent projects. One is the neoconservative approach that seeks to reconstruct the world system by democratizing all the states within it (if necessary at the point of a gun). The other is cosmopolitan democracy, seeking to extend the tradition of multilateral construction of formal international institutions, with the idea of making them not just more powerful, but also more responsive to popular control on the part of the peoples of the world. I try to show that discursive democracy is both more feasible and more attractive than these alternatives.

Preface

I begin in chapter 1 by describing the trend from single and dominant to multiple and contested discourses in key areas of the international system: international political economy, international security, human rights, the global environment, and the politics of identity. Chapters 2–4 take on some of the most severe and intractable conflicts in the contemporary divided world. Chapter 2 reinterprets the alleged clash of civilizations as portrayed by Samuel Huntington and others as a number of clashes across discourses. This seeming clash of civilizations is in reality just an illustration of the degree to which international conflict is the result of contending discourses, some of which can be captured in "civilizational" terms, some of which cannot be so captured. This contestation can provide grist for deliberative engagement in transnational public spheres – not just the hostility which Huntington believes can only be managed by civilizational elites in top-down fashion. Chapter 3 looks at violent conflicts of ethnic, religious, and national identity in deeply divided societies, again showing how such identities are the construction of discourses, and how engagement across discourses at a distance from the construction of sovereign authority can constitute a deliberative and democratic as well as an effective response to identity conflicts. Chapter 4 examines international terrorism in light of its conflictual discourse aspects. These aspects are recognized by those prosecuting the so-called "war on terror" (itself a particular discourse construction) in the United States and elsewhere. However, these discourse aspects are often treated in simplistic and ultimately counterproductive terms as a matter for a "war of ideas" against ideologies sympathetic to terrorism, or for the exercise of "soft power" alongside military force. I show that the insecure world that exists in the wake of the September 11, 2001 attacks and the war in Iraq is amenable to a more democratic engagement across discourses. This engagement could help reconstruct global governance and so combat the global insecurity created by both terrorists and those who oppose them in such crude fashion.

Preface

Chapter 5 turns to the international political economy, and especially the extent to which globalization signals a decline in the capacity of states and other entities to exercise authority on an autonomous basis. This chapter explores the prospects for a more deliberative globalization as an alternative to the dominance of market liberalism. Sometimes economic globalization and its market liberal discourse can look like a monolith; but there are cracks, internal tensions, and oppositions to globalization that enable more transnationally democratic possibilities. Effective navigation of a globalizing world demands a particular kind of reflexive intelligence that attends to how actions both proceed within and help recreate situations, whose character is outlined in chapter 6. I show that this sort of reflexive action is hardest for states, somewhat easier for corporations, and most straightforward for civil society actors unencumbered by the imperatives and constraints that burden states and corporations. Diffuse reflexive action in which civil society actors and activists figure centrally points to a democratic politics featuring widespread ability to influence the configuration of discourses in the international system. Resistance in the form of social movement protest has a part to play in this process, be it against corporate globalization, or against war. Paradoxically, resistance can help produce order as well as disruption in the system. Reflexivity and resistance contribute to discursive democratization. This project has many of the same foes (such as unilateralism and violent conflict) as a project of much longer standing: liberal multilateralism.

Chapter 7 shows that liberal multilateralism is increasingly problematic in a complex and divided world. Its formal institutional solutions are especially prone to the hazards of excessive constitutionalization and excessive administration of international affairs, risking dominance of formal rules and rigid bureaucratic structures. These responses are inadequate in an interdependent, complex, networked world of contested discourses. I conclude in chapter 8 with a comparison of discursive democracy and its two most visible rivals when it comes to extending democracy in the international system:

neoconservatism and the extension of multilateralism found in cosmopolitan democracy.

The idea for this book came originally at a conference, "Democracy After Governance," organized by Henrik Bang at the University of Copenhagen in 2003. Since then, aspects of it have been presented at the Conference on Deliberative Democracy and Sensitive Issues, University of Amsterdam, 2003; the Department of International Relations and Social and Political Theory Program, both at Australian National University; the Department of Political Science at the University of Utah; the Centre for Theoretical Studies at the University of Essex; the Department of Political Science at the University of North Carolina; the Symposium on Human Rights, Global Justice, and Cosmopolitan Democracy at the University of Queensland, 2005; and the 2005 Conference of the American Political Science Association. Aside from audiences at these locations, I have benefited from advice and criticism from Tjitske Akkerman, Daniele Archibugi, Jeffrey Berejikian, James Bohman, Molly Cochran, Robyn Eckersley, John Forester, Nancy Fraser, Bruno Frey, Carol Gould, David Howarth, Bora Kanra, Ilan Kapoor, Chandran Kukathas, Stephen Leonard, Christian List, Gerry Mackie, David Marsh, Anthony McGrew, Kathy Morton, Anne McNevin, Claus Offe, Benjamin Reilly, Geoffrey Stokes, Mark Warren, Albert Weale, Iris Young, and two anonymous readers for Polity Press.

I have used some of the text from three previously published articles:

Jeffrey Berejikian and John S. Dryzek, "Reflexive Action in International Politics," *British Journal of Political Science* 30 (2000): 193–216. Reprinted by permission of Cambridge University Press. A small portion of this paper is used in chapter 6.

John S. Dryzek, "Deliberative Democracy in Divided Societies: Alternatives to Agonism and Analgesia," *Political Theory* 33 (2005): 218–42. Reprinted by permission of Sage Publications. This paper forms the basis of chapter 3.

John S. Dryzek, "Transnational Democracy in an Insecure World," *International Political Science Review* 27 (2006). Reprinted by permission of the International Political Science Association and Sage Publications. The text from this paper is drawn on in several places, notably in chapter 4.

1

Welcome to a Divided World

A World of Discourses

Many of the conflicts in today's international system can most fruitfully be interpreted as clashes of discourses. I will explore reasons for an increase in the relative incidence of discourse clashes in recent years. While recognizing the dark side of these contemporary developments, I will also show that discourses can engage as well as clash, and that unprecedented democratic possibilities can also be found in this engagement if one looks hard enough. These possibilities can be linked to some contemporary thinking about deliberative democracy, which has begun to take on the challenges posed by the international system.

A discourse is a shared set of concepts, categories, and ideas that provides its adherents with a framework for making sense of situations, embodying judgments, assumptions, capabilities, dispositions, and intentions. It provides basic terms for analysis, debates, agreements, and disagreements. Its language enables individuals who subscribe to it to compile the bits of information they receive into coherent accounts organized around storylines that can be shared in intersubjectively meaningful ways. Important discourses that will be visited in subsequent chapters include:

- *Market liberalism*, the dominant global economic discourse that emphasizes free trade, capital mobility, and deregulation.

- *Globalization*, highlighting the increasing intensity of international social, economic, and political interactions, and the degree to which systems are increasingly organized at the global level, eluding control by sovereign states.

- *Anti-corporate globalization*, an emerging counter-discourse that challenges economic globalization, incorporating a variety of local and justice concerns.

- *Realism*, long central in international diplomacy and foreign policy, taking the world as an anarchy at the edge of violence, where states must strategize with and against each other to maximize their own security.

- *Human Rights*, stressing a basic set of rights that individuals everywhere can claim, and which states and international institutions ought to uphold and respect.

- *Counter-terror*, which would subordinate human rights and sovereignty to security, at least when it comes to dealing with those branded as actual or potential terrorists and their supporters.

- *Neoconservatism*, which shot to prominence in the United States after 2001, rejecting realism in favor of an idealism that believed peace could be secured by making countries liberal, capitalist, and democratic.

- *Industrialism*, long taken for granted in capitalist and communist countries alike, stressing material growth driven by technological progress as the highest aspiration, denying ecological constraints on human progress.

- *Sustainable development*, the dominant discourse on global environmental affairs since the mid-1980s, stressing collective action to secure mutually reinforcing values of environmental protection, justice within and between generations, and economic growth.

- *Discourses of identity*, defined on the basis of religion, ethnicity, or "civilization."

Welcome to a Divided World

Discourses construct meaning, distinguish agents (with the capacity to take effective action) from those who can only be acted upon, establish relations between actors and others, delimit what counts as legitimate knowledge, and define common sense (Milliken, 1999). Discourses are a matter of practice as well as words, for actions in the social realm are always accompanied by language that establishes the meaning of action. So practices help constitute, reconstitute, and sometimes challenge discourses. Even something as simple as presenting a passport at immigration control helps reinforce the discourse of sovereignty. Discourses can embody power in that they condition norms and perceptions of actors, suppressing some interests while advancing others.[1] Discourses pervade, constitute, and help explain the structure of international affairs. The power of discourses arises in their ability to structure and coordinate the actions of individuals subject wholly or partly to them. This coordination can apply to individuals who otherwise have no formal relationship in that they never meet face to face, are not part of the same organization or same state, and have no direct interaction.[2]

Once, divisions in the international system were constituted mostly by rival states confronting one another. Sometimes those confrontations took place between alliances (such as NATO and the Warsaw Pact). Sometimes states expanded into empires, though this became less fashionable as the twentieth century progressed. Sometimes rivalry led to war. At other times states could find a way to construct international institutions that curbed violence and produced more peaceful coexistence. States could be riven internally by conflicts between social classes, which occasionally spilled over into international politics, especially when during the Cold War the Soviet Union or United States took an interest in one or other of the sides in a class conflict.

Today's world is different. War between states is rare. Class conflicts that do still exist seldom become internationalized. Violent conflict still exists, but violence occurs more often in civil wars, or between networks that transcend national boundaries, involving armies but also guerrillas and other unofficial participants. Division is largely a matter of identity; sometimes defined in a fashion that coincides with the accepted boundaries of a nation-state, but more often not. Identity can be a matter of religion or ethnicity as well as nationality, and receives especially forceful expression in the presence of others who subscribe to an opposing identity. Sometimes identity is defined mainly in terms of local opposition to a dominant entity, be it the sole remaining superpower or the globalized market economy. Identities are not primordial or given; they are constructed by discourses.

Ignorance or denigration of the importance of this discourse dimension of action is not just a matter of oversight on the part of observers and analysts. Rather, it can be a tragic mistake on the part of policy-makers whose actions go seriously wrong as they take effect in a world of discourses, and often produce exactly the opposite result of that intended. In subsequent chapters I will point to occasions where these actions produce war instead of peace, chaos instead of order, danger instead of security, death instead of life. Recognition of the discourse dimension is therefore not simply a matter of analytical perspicacity; it is also a matter of being able to act intelligently in a dangerous world. There are lessons here for all international actors, be they superpowers, mid-ranking states, non-governmental organizations (NGOs), corporations, or even terrorists.

Discourses and Other Stuff

Whether looking at negotiations, international organizations, coercive diplomacy, armed conflict, markets, or international law, many analysts of international conflict believe that it is the strategies of states and other actors that are the most important factors that determine what kind of order exists and the sorts of outcomes that are generated. This kind of approach pervades international relations and its study. It is strengthened by the recent popularity of rational choice-based models of politics, which take from economics the assumption that actors are rational maximizers of their utility, then look at what happens when such actors interact in political settings ranging from negotiations to armed conflicts.

Yet social interaction, including international interaction, is a linguistic as well as strategic activity. At one level this is already recognized, even by strategists who study the most militarized aspects of international relations. After all, deployment of an aircraft carrier or regiment is normally accompanied by words that explain what the deployment means and what it is intended to accomplish. Threats and inducements directed at adversaries (or allies) themselves come in the form of language. When "jaw, jaw" displaces "war, war" (in Winston Churchill's words) and adversaries meet at the negotiating table, again their strategic encounter takes place using words. The hard-headed strategist – for example, a game theorist – would say that words are just cheap talk, the medium through which the deeper structure of the inter-action proceeds. But even such a hard nut would have to concede that the underlying conception of the game is itself constituted by a linguistic understanding among the players (Risse, 2000). This underlying conception would begin with recognition that there really is a game, and extend to what kind of game it is – zero-sum (when one side can only gain at the other's expense), positive sum (where joint gains are available), adversarial, mixed motive, etc.

Those with hopes for the multilateral construction of institutions to curb conflict in the international system sometimes analyze negotiations that construct these institutions and subsequent decisions in terms of rational strategic calculations by actors. For example, the United States signed off on the 1987 Montreal Protocol for the protection of the ozone layer only after realizing that its chemical companies were well placed to profit from manufacturing alternatives to the CFCs restricted by the Protocol. Strategy can also inform the rational calculus of actors as they decide whether or not to comply with agreements, or on the terms of their compliance. Yet discourse still matters: the discourse that defined the ozone problem to begin with also gave a particular kind of role to science within the negotiations. As Litfin (1994) demonstrates, strategic interactions do not explain the successful outcome of the negotiations, because positions only shifted in favor of an agreement with the rhetorical force of the idea of an "ozone hole" in the Southern hemisphere. Litfin shows that agreement on the Protocol required a shift to a discourse of precaution that highlighted risks from ozone layer depletion.

Negotiations of this sort often combine strategic action and mutual understandings constructed by language. Sometimes that language will be given by taken-for-granted discourses. When it comes to environmental issues like ozone, the discourse of sustainable development under which "precaution" can be subsumed can be particularly powerful, as it combines economic and environmental values. Sometimes participants may, as a result of reflection induced by communication, be open to changing their minds; this is where deliberation enters the picture. Deliberative theorists generally contrast strategic action with communicative action. Strategic action involves individuals and other actors calculating what best serves their established goals. In communicative action, individuals seek mutual understanding and are prepared to reflect upon the content of their interests (Habermas, 1984), and upon the discourses in which those interests are embedded.

When it comes to the international political economy, impersonal market forces rather than discourses are often emphasized. If policy-makers do not respond in the right way to these forces, they will be punished by markets in the form of disinvestment, capital flight, and pressure on their currency. But the fact that policy-makers believe these consequences will follow is a result of the influence of a particular discourse (market liberalism) over them. Other economic actors are themselves attuned to market liberal discourse. So (for example) if a government makes a policy decision to expand its welfare state or increase protection against imports, financiers anticipating a negative reaction in international markets will pull their funds out of the government's currency, and corporations will cancel their investment plans. So as not to be caught out themselves, these actors will initiate the punishment. The prophecy becomes self-fulfilling, causing the results whose anticipation was the reason for actions. The impersonal forces of the market take effect because of the subscription of market actors and policy-makers to market liberal discourse.

Now, recognition of the pervasive importance of discourses in conditioning the world is not new. However, discourses have generally had their stories told in terms of how they have conditioned and ordered the international system as a whole – they are treated as singular and universal, "hegemonic" in terms of how they condition interactions, not multiple and contested. A discourse is hegemonic if it has no serious rivals, such that it becomes ingrained in the understanding of all relevant actors, defining their common sense and conditioning their interactions.[3] Hegemonic discourses can serve some interests and oppress others.

When it comes to the international system, the content of hegemonic discourses can and does change with time. For example, Reus-Smit (1999) tells the story of how social constructions of "sovereignty" have changed over time; sovereignty was constructed very differently in the international system of ancient Greek city-states from how it has been in the modern world. In the Middle Ages sovereignty hardly existed, as feudal lords would claim authority against each other and against their king, often using violence to press their claims (Teschke, 1997). For Reus-Smit, variations in the content of sovereignty over time have been consistent with different views of the moral purpose of the state – for example, the absolutist state of seventeenth- and eighteenth-century Europe had as its moral purpose the upholding of divinely sanctioned social hierarchy. Since then, the state's moral purpose has involved facilitating human potential, especially when it comes to economic activity. But at any one time a single conception of sovereignty generally dominates.[4]

To take another example of the telling of discourse stories in unitary terms, in the early nineteenth century European colonial powers ruled empires that spanned the globe. But communications from the colony to the capital could take months in either direction. The power of the metropolitan center was secured largely on the basis of the shared cultural understandings of colonial administrators. For example, the "Hellenistic" ethos (based on an idealized view of how Ancient Athens conducted its imperial affairs) assimilated by British administrators in Australia enabled "governing at a distance" (Kendal, 1997).

Truly hegemonic discourses are so ingrained that they are not even recognized by those subject to them, but are instead treated as part of the natural order of things. Patriarchy has been like this in many societies until the rise of feminism enabled it to be recognized, named, and resisted. Industrialism – the taken-for-granted desirability and inevitability of technological change and economic growth – again was so pervasive and hegemonic as to be unrecognized until the rise of environmentalism since the late 1960s enabled it to be named and questioned. Many of those influenced by Michel Foucault's historical accounts of discourses write in these terms, of discourses so pervasive and powerful, they are unrecognized and so inescapable. When Foucault's ideas have been extended into the study of international relations, the intent has often been to portray an oppressive hegemonic totality in which the academic study of international relations is itself complicit (George, 1994; Walker, 1993). Realism, the long dominant understanding of foreign policy-makers and academic analysts alike, has often been seen in these terms.

From Hegemony to Contestation

In contrast to these popular depictions of discourse hegemony, a look around today's world reveals some important discourse contests. Consider the following examples of discourse hegemony turning into discourse contestation.

International political economy

Since the early 1980s, international economic affairs have been dominated by the "Washington Consensus," a set of understandings about the desirability of free trade, capital mobility, and deregulated markets, rooted in a discourse of market liberalism. The assumptions, understandings, scripts, and remedies of market liberalism now pervade international economic and financial systems, providing actors with cues about how to act, to reward actions on behalf of free trade, deregulation, and capital mobility, and to punish actions that impede these values. These constraints were always implicit in the logic of market systems, such that governments that defied them could expect stormy weather. But since the early 1980s, it has become ever harder for any government to defy the Washington Consensus. The reason is that the Consensus is now accepted by most key actors in the world economic system. This acceptance is not just, or even mainly, on the part of centralized police officers such as the World Trade Organization (WTO), International Monetary Fund (IMF), or US government. Instead, it pervades the myriad investors and financiers who immediately punish a government that departs from the market liberal recipe.

The Confucian capitalist countries of East Asia once had an exemption from the Washington Consensus, their economic development secured by an interventionist state in cooperation with large corporations. All this changed with the Asian economic crisis of 1997. The relationships once praised as cooperative business–government partnerships were now denounced as corrupt "crony capitalism," and so a rival economic development model to the Washington Consensus was demolished (Hall, 2003). The contest was essentially a clash between two discourses, with market liberalism coming out on top – with some continued resistance (e.g., from Malaysia, which did not adopt IMF prescriptions in the wake of the crisis).

The market liberalism of the Washington Consensus has been further strengthened by its expression in a discourse of economic globalization. Globalization refers to increasing intensity of many kinds of interactions across territorial boundaries, not just economic ones (see chapter 5). Globalization as an economic discourse highlights the degree to which economic integration is occurring, downplaying evidence of persistent national boundaries and differences in public policies, implying that governments have no alternative when it comes to public policy. They must adjust to economic reality as defined by market liberalism, and so (for example) dismantle expensive welfare states (Hay, 1998).

This history – of market liberalism defeating the East Asian model, and strengthened further by its expression in globalization – might seem to be a case of a discourse securing an ever more hegemonic grip on the international system. But we can also see contestation. Beginning in the late 1990s there emerged a competitor in the form of a transnational discourse formed from a series of localized resistances to market liberalism. Protests against the world economic order, beginning in Seattle in 1999, initially baffled observers attuned not just to the benefits of this order, but also to conventional ways of thinking about political movements. The protestors had no common program, let alone any intention to seize or even seek a share in political power. Many of their concerns seemed contradictory. It was not even clear that the label "anti-globalization" was really appropriate, given that the protestors did not reject all aspects of globalization (especially those facilitating the organization of transnational advocacy networks). Its members often prefer the label "global justice" (Burgmann, 2003, suggests the term "anti-corporate globalization movement"). These protests were struggles over meaning: to challenge the assumption that global economic growth can be equated with progress, to attach negative connotations to brands such as Nike and McDonalds,[5] and so open space for recognition of varieties of local struggles against international economic regimes or particular corporations. They could make common cause with skeptics such as Hirst and Thompson (1996), who pointed to the degree of autonomy that states still had in resisting the demands of corporate globalization, and former World Bank Chief Economist Joseph Stiglitz (2002) who criticized market liberal recipes. This counter-discourse eventually made its presence felt in the deliberations of international economic institutions (see chapter 6). Economic globalization itself began to be recognized as a discourse whose "logic of no alternative" was itself a social construction that served a particular political agenda, but could in fact be challenged (Hay, 1998). This challenge was felt both within states and in the development of modes of globalization that involved governance and political interaction, not just market liberalization.

International security

A "realist" understanding of international conflict has long been the staple of international security affairs. Realism assumes that the international system is populated by states that are organized internally as hierarchies, but have little in the way of formal rules and institutions to govern their interactions. The international system itself is treated as an anarchy, a potentially hostile environment where violence is an ever-present possibility. There is no room for sentiment, only hard-headed calculation in the interests of securing the safety and comparative advantage of one's own state. Former US Secretary of State Henry Kissinger is perhaps the political leader who in recent decades subscribed to realist tenets most comprehensively, but many other policy-makers subscribe to a greater or lesser degree. Realism as a school of thought pervades the academic study of international relations, though not without dispute. "Neorealism" as set out by Waltz (1979) stresses that it is the structure of anarchy in the system that forces states to pursue self-help and military advantage, and to make strategic decisions about alliances and conflicts with security as their uppermost concern.[6]

But as Wendt (1992) points out, "anarchy is what states make of it." That is, anarchy of this Hobbesian sort – at the edge of chaos and violence – only exists to the degree key policy-makers in states believe it does. (Though, in its more technical sense anarchy as a political system lacking a sovereign entity like the state is an undeniable fact of the international system.) Realism grounded in Hobbesian anarchy is, then, a discourse, and as such is sustained by the understandings and practices of the actors participating in it.

11

Thus it is not an immutable deep structure of the kind neo-realists portray. This shared understanding was long the received wisdom among policy-makers and intellectuals in security affairs. However, a more idealistic view of the international system long believed that anarchy could be curbed and order promoted by the development of international institutions (see chapter 7). The institutions in question might include the United Nations (UN) and its agencies, the World Bank, the IMF, as well as treaties, international regimes, and cooperative agreements between states. The "English School" in international relations treats the international system as a society of states, which together create rules and norms to guide their interactions (Bull, 1977), producing order without recourse to strong global institutions (Keal, 2000: 68).

The discourse of anarchy has come in for some major challenges in recent decades. In the 1980s a major challenge came from Soviet leader Mikhail Gorbachev. Why did the Cold War end? In part because Gorbachev's "new thinking" simply redefined the nature of the relationship between East and West in terms that did not have to be adversarial: "these ideas *were* the Cold War, and as such changing them by definition changed the reality" (Wendt, 1999: 375).

After 2001, Wendt's insight about the social construction of anarchy was confirmed from a very different direction. The challenge came from neoconservatives in the US government, who believed that anarchy could be changed by imposing liberal democracy and a capitalist market economy on states in the world system. This imposition would proceed by conquering, reforming, or cowing states opposing the United States. Neoconservatives are much more idealistic than realists. They believe other states can be made more peaceful and less of a threat by turning them into liberal democracies in the Western image. On the "democratic peace" thesis, first proposed more than 200 years ago by Immanuel Kant, democracies do not go to war with each other (for evidence, see Russett and Oneal, 2001: 81–124).

However important it may be in driving US policy in Iraq and elsewhere, neoconservatism is unlike the discourse of realism and anarchy because it is not a shared understanding that provides a context for interaction across national boundaries. It is confined to policy-makers, intellectuals, and publications in one state, and targets in the first instance the policies of that state alone, though it is interested in having other states fall into line. Beyond this it plays little role in systemic coordination, because few other actors, even US allies, come close to accepting it. Neoconservatives are not deterred by this lack of acceptance, believing that the United States does not need partners in order to bring deviant states into line. They might accept tactical support such as that provided by the United Kingdom, Poland, and Australia in the Iraq war, but that support is not motivated by a shared zeal for democratization. While the discourse anticipates a world of capitalist democracies at peace with one another, until that day arrives neoconservatism is a highly disruptive force in international security affairs.

Realists argue that whether states are liberal democracies or not is irrelevant, as states will always have to be guided in their actions by their strategic interests. The realist discourse of anarchy did not completely give way to neoconservatism, even within the United States; indeed, US realists were among the opponents of neoconservative military adventure in Iraq.

The defining feature of international security at the dawn of the twenty-first century was a "war on terror" led by the United States. The war on terror is a quintessentially discourse-based conflict. The whole idea of a war on *terror* implies an adversary that is a concept, not a physical entity like an opposing state or its army that can be confronted on the ground and defeated in tangible terms. Describing the situation as a *war* was a choice that did not have to be made (and other countries such as the UK facing the IRA and Spain facing ETA have dealt with terrorists without constructing a "war"). The "war" proclamation served all kinds of purposes for the George W. Bush administration – not least its re-election in 2004, as sufficient numbers of Americans were frightened by the specter of terror to cast their fortunes with a Bush presidency. But the *war* designation served positive purposes for Islamic terrorists too – by constructing them as warriors rather than criminals.

The adversary became still more elusive in the construction of US Secretary of Defense Donald Rumsfeld. In a June 2002 press conference, Rumsfeld referred to "unknown unknowns," "the things we don't know we don't know" to which the United States must nevertheless respond in pre-emptive fashion. By definition, any challenge from an "unknown unknown" is short on tangible evidence. The shortfall is made up for with assumptions and suppositions that can only be the product of a discourse. On the other side, al-Qaeda is coordinated not as a hierarchy, not even really as a network, but rather as a discourse. In chapter 4 I will detail the ways in which al-Qaeda as a discourse is in part the unintended consequence of actions taken by United States policy-makers. For in nominating al-Qaeda as its number one adversary, the United States government and its media supporters provide massive incentives for any terrorist group or individual to claim the al-Qaeda mantle. In an odd way, the aftermath of 9/11 was a triumph of postmodernism, as labels created things.

Human rights to counter-terror

Central to the rights discourse is a basic range of human rights to which all individuals in the world are entitled. The discourse's pre-eminence was confirmed in the Universal Declaration of Human Rights adopted by the United Nations in 1948. The precise content and relative weight of rights has often been disputed within the discourse. For example, are there rights to basic human needs such as shelter, food, and education? If so, how important are they compared to private property rights? Should the commitment to freedom of expression and association be absolute? Such internal disputes did not shake the rights discourse itself, and even while countries (including the Soviet Union) systematically violated individual rights in practice, they claimed adherence to the basic idea of human rights itself. This hypocrisy could itself be turned to good use by human rights activists attempting to make states practice what they preached.

Eventually, however, the rights discourse saw a challenge from those who saw it as a Western imposition. Prime Minister Lee Kwan Yew of Singapore was particularly vociferous in stressing "Asian values" of community and consensus against the divisive individualism he saw in the human rights discourse. Later, the West itself wavered in its commitment to the rights discourse. After the attacks on the World Trade Center and Pentagon on September 11, 2001, Islamic extremism and the violence it validated were met by a discourse of counter-terror. Formalized in the *National Security Strategy of the United States of America* in September 2002 as a doctrine of prevention and pre-emption, this discourse licensed states (such as Russia, Israel, the Philippines) to override human rights considerations in the fight against opponents who could now more securely be branded as actual or potential terrorists. Those so branded could then be treated as beyond the reach of the Geneva Convention and Universal Declaration of Human Rights, to be imprisoned without due process and subjected to torture. The United States itself treated suspects like this, in Guantanamo Bay and Abu Ghraib prison in Iraq.

The doctrine of "prevention and pre-emption" also modified established notions of sovereignty by making it conditional on not being considered likely to support terrorism against the United States and its allies. (Actually supporting terrorism would have been disallowed under long-established sovereignty norms.) Under the states system established by the Treaty of Westphalia in 1648, sovereignty meant that a state could act more or less as it liked within its boundaries – within limits. As Krasner (1999) points out, this has never meant complete impunity, and the sovereignty norm has often been violated in practice. Those at the receiving end of colonialism found little protection in the sovereignty norm (Keene, 2002). In the recent past, sovereignty has become still more conditional on behaving according to some external norms, defined recently by the

counter-terror discourse, prior to that by the idea of "humanitarian intervention" whereby outsiders could intervene
militarily to protect oppressed populations (as for example in
Kosovo in the late 1990s). "Humanitarian intervention" can
be consistent with and reinforce the rights discourse (though
skeptics would also see it as another way for dominant Western states to impose their will); "counter-terror" undermines
the rights discourse.

The question of who exactly is a terrorist and so beyond
the reach of the rights discourse is constructed by the discourse of counter-terror (and its antecedents). Some
perpetrators of violence are defined in, others defined out.
Over time, Mujahideen, once armed by the West and praised
as freedom fighters by US presidents in the context of Cold
War struggles in Afghanistan, became redefined as terrorists,
now likely to be pursued and killed rather than praised. States
and their leaders could also undergo such reclassification.
Saddam Hussein's regime in Iraq actually used weapons of
mass destruction in poison gas attacks on Iranians and Kurds
in the 1980s. But as the regime was seen as a bulwark against
Islamic fundamentalism in Iran, such misbehavior was generally ignored by the West. The retrospective reclassification of
the regime's 1980s actions as evil only came about when
these interests no longer coincided. The discourse of counter-
terror treated such wrongdoers not as violators of the rights of
others and so requiring the administration of international
justice. Rather, they were constructed as evil-doers who did
not merit due process and the protection that the rights discourse provides. In short, human rights and counter-terror
became contending discourses.

The global environment:
industrialism to sustainable development and beyond

The term "environment" did not exist prior to the late 1960s.
The dominant discourse in what we now name and recognize
as global environmental affairs was up until that point industrialism – though it could not even be named, because it was
so taken for granted as the natural order of things. Industrial-

ism sees growing material economic prosperity fueled by technological progress as the highest good, and does not recognize any global limits to economic growth or any ecological constraints on human activity. From an environmental perspective, liberalism, conservatism, fascism, democratic socialism, and Marxism are really all just variations on a theme of industrialism.

Industrialism came into focus with the arrival of environmentalism in the late 1960s. In the 1970s global environmental concern was framed mostly in terms of the idea that there were finite global stocks of natural resources and ecological boundaries to human activity – the "limits to growth" (Meadows et al., 1972). This discourse of limits and survival yielded in the 1980s to one of sustainable development, confirmed in 1987 by the Brundtland Report to the UN, *Our Common Future* (see Lafferty, 1996). Sustainable development denies that global limits act as fixed constraints, for they can be avoided through intelligent collective action. Economic growth, environmental protection, social justice, and intergenerational equity are seen as mutually reinforcing – though again intelligent collective action is required, and positive results will not be achieved automatically. Sustainable development is nowhere an accomplished fact, nor is it entirely clear how we would recognize it if it were. The concept remains disputed, and large corporations (organized into the World Business Council for Sustainable Development) have tried with some success to bend it in a business-friendly direction. Sustainable development should be treated as a discourse, not a concept capable of precise definition (Dryzek, 2005: ch. 7). This discourse has dominated international environmental affairs, from the UN Conference on Environment and Development in Rio in 1992 to the World Summit on Sustainable Development in Johannesburg in 2002 and beyond.

However, the sustainable development discourse still battles a limits discourse which never quite went away, now revived by those who stress the threat of global warming, and the need to curb global emissions of greenhouse gases in order to avert ecological catastrophe. The limits discourse was never actually disproved by sustainable development; its main problem was perhaps that it was just too unpalatable to drive policy action in a world where economic growth was so central (Torgerson, 1995). In a different direction, sustainable development also battles a resurgent industrialism. Industrialism is given a Promethean twist by those such as Bjørn Lomborg (2001) who attempt to debunk environmentalism by showing that global indicators of human wellbeing are all pointing in the right direction. Prometheans argue that pollution is falling, and natural resources are becoming more plentiful with time (as a result of human ingenuity harnessed by the capitalist system). Prometheans can make common cause with market liberalism, especially in the US presidencies of Ronald Reagan and George W. Bush, and license US opposition to global environmental agreements such as the Kyoto Protocol on climate change. This discourse coalition is given added force by the WTO, which, operating under market liberalism, interprets environmental protection measures taken by national governments (for example, specifying that imported fish be caught without endangering marine mammals) as restraints on trade that must be overruled. Different again, green radicals challenge sustainable development on the grounds of its accommodation with established systems of power and economic priorities, for being far too moderate in any conceivable response to ecological crisis.

In short, this environmental example illustrates a realm of global human activity that went from the uncontested hegemony of the discourse of industrialism until the 1960s to a situation of contestation and engagement across multiple discourses in subsequent decades.[7]

The "clash of civilizations" and the politics of identity

With the attacks on the World Trade Center and Pentagon on September 11, 2001, the idea of a "clash of civilizations" gained added force. According to Samuel Huntington (1993, 1996), the clash of ideologies (liberalism versus Marxism) that defined the Cold War is replaced by a more complex set of conflicts across the world's main civilizational blocks (Western, Islamic, Orthodox, Hindu, "Sinic," Buddhist, Japanese, African, and Latin American civilizations). Huntington believes that the rise of these conflicts is facilitated by the increasing intensity of interactions across civilizational boundaries that accompanies modernization (not to be confused with Westernization). Relatedly, the 1990s also saw a resurgent politics of identity, though not all such identities are "civilizational" in Huntington's terms. Sometimes this politics was relatively peaceful, but occasionally it became murderous – especially when a particular ethnic, religious, or national identity was expressed in terms whose validation required suppression of another identity. The worst was seen in the former Yugoslavia, in parts of the former Soviet Union, and in Rwanda.

In chapters 2 and 3 I will argue that both the alleged clash of civilizations and the politics of identity that characterizes divided societies can best be interpreted as clashes of discourses. That is, these conflicts have their roots in the way particular discourses construct identity, not in any primordial history, and certainly not in genetics that define different peoples. The relevant discourses would include the radical anti-Western discourse that gained ground in the Islamic world in the 1990s, receiving violent expression in the actions of Osama bin Laden and al-Qaeda, but also more localized national and ethnic identities.

Reasons for Increasing Conflict

In all these cases – international political economy, international security, human rights to counter-terror, the environment, the clash of civilizations, the politics of identity in divided societies – the movement is from discourse hegemony to discourse conflict. Is this simply a matter of coincidence, or is something deeper afoot?

There are common underlying processes at work. Despite the fact that he is wrong about so much (or so I will argue in

19

chapter 2), Huntington is actually on the right track when he identifies modernization as one of the culprits in explaining intensification in the alleged clash of civilizations. However, modernization to Huntington is mostly a matter of improved communications and economic interactions (i.e., globalization). Another aspect of modernization is growing critical awareness of hitherto taken-for-granted influences on one's life, and a corresponding ability to question the traditions in which one has been socialized.

Throughout much if not most of human history, the majority of people have been socialized within particular traditions that have generally reinforced the disciplining power of hegemonic discourses. This is the kind of history portrayed by Michel Foucault and his followers. Truly powerful discourses are so ingrained that they are not even recognized by their adherents. The discourses in question might concern sanity, sexuality, criminality, economics, religion, government, and politics. What they had in common was the power to transform some contingent understandings into taken-for-granted truths, the seeming natural order of things, so pervasive and powerful as to be inescapable. Those sorts of understandings have become increasingly subject to critical scrutiny; this is what Giddens calls the "de-traditionalization" of societies (see Beck et al., 1994). De-traditionalization can refer to the loss of authority of religious and mythical traditions; but it extends too to some thoroughly modern traditions – such as traditions that saw economic growth and technological progress as both inevitable and right (the discourse of industrialism). Beck et al. describe "reflexive modernization," under which individuals in society become increasingly questioning of the social bases on which society is built (though these authors do not use the "discourse" terminology). Their narrative points in the direction of enlightenment. However, increased awareness of the availability of discourses other than the ones in which one has been socialized does not necessarily point in the direction of reflection, tolerance, and enlightenment. It can have exactly the opposite effect, by instilling a sense of threat on the part of adherents of a tradition who now realize that there are powerful alternatives to it. Indeed, this sort of reaction pretty much defines religious fundamentalisms, be they Christian, Islamic, Hindu, or Jewish, as they react to the modern and globalizing world. We can call this "reflexive traditionalization."

A very rough accounting of discourses strengthened and undermined by processes of reflexive modernization and reflexive traditionalization is presented in table 1.1. Reflexive modernization facilitates discourses that arise to question dominant understandings and practices. So anti-corporate globalization questions the global political economy and market liberalism; neoconservatism challenges the established order of realism and anarchy; limits and survival questions industrialism; and eventually sustainable development raises a host of questions about the way social, economic, and ecological systems work. Reflexive traditionalization strengthens discourses that reaffirm the identity of one's own side and reject some vilified other. Religious fundamentalisms, ethnic, national, and civilizational discourses, and counter-terror all fall into this category. Correspondingly, reflexive traditionalization undermines universalistic discourses such as human rights and liberalism. While one could argue about some of the placements in this table, the general point is that few of the discourses underwriting order and conflict in today's world discussed earlier in this chapter are untouched.

Table 1.1 Effects of reflexive modernization and traditionalization

	Reflexive modernization	Reflexive traditionalization
Strengthens:	Anti-corporate globalization	Religious fundamentalisms
	Neoconservatism	Ethnic and national identities
	Limits and survival	"Civilizational" identities
	Sustainable development	Counter-terror
Undermines:	Market liberalism	Human rights
	Anarchy/realism	Liberalism
	Confucian capitalism	
	Industrialism	

From Discourse Contestation to Discursive Democracy

The increased possibility of reflective choices in the context of awareness of a variety of discourses can take us beyond the accounts of those at the "critical" end of international relations scholarship who have emphasized the disciplining power of hegemonic discourses in the international system. Beyond occasional homage to resistance, these sorts of analysts tend to neglect practices that might change the configuration of discourses for better or worse (see Neumann, 2002, for criticism of this tendency). Discourse analysts who follow the tradition of Michel Foucault are often reluctant to say what if anything can be done to counter the influence of the oppressive discourses they identify (beyond destabilization), let alone refashion them. Constructivist analysts of international relations (e.g, Ruggie, 1998; Wendt, 1999) are not necessarily so harsh on each and every discourse. They are mostly concerned to identify the historical contingency of concepts such as sovereignty and anarchy, showing that they are in truth social constructions of intersubjective beliefs that change over time. But one of the standard criticisms of constructivists used to be that in emphasizing the causal force of structures, they lacked a theory of agency. That is, they failed to say how, why, and when actors can change the terms of the norms, structures, and concepts that constitute the international system (Checkel, 1988).

Constructivists are correct in identifying the pervasive and changeable constitutive power of language in international relations. Discourses can sometimes have the pervasive and oppressive character that followers of Foucault often attribute to them. However, for reasons I have explained, discourses and their contestation can also be treated as increasingly amenable to influence from the reflective choices of human agents. Indeed, it is because of the potential for such choices becoming consequential in the contemporary world, including the international system, that the extent of the importance of discourses for intelligent action becomes apparent. The possibilities for such action are actually enhanced to the degree postmodernists are right in their core claim that we are witnessing the dissolution of the meta-narratives (science, instrumental-analytic rationality, progress, individualism) that defined the modern era.

These possibilities for critical interchange in the engagement of proliferating discourses open the door to some major opportunities for introducing democracy into the international system. For much of its history, thinking about democracy has been confined to the level of the sovereign state, or sub-units such as local government, responsive only to the people within a state's boundaries. But as states have become increasingly subject to authority in the international system – organized by regional bodies such as the European Union (EU), or global institutions such as the WTO and IMF – interest has grown in democratizing the international system itself. Global bodies such as the WTO, IMF, and even the UN are currently not at all democratic. The EU is only slightly better, for though it has an elected parliament, its power is limited, and the EU is widely perceived as suffering from a "democratic deficit" when compared to the degree of democracy obtaining in its member states.

The basic justification for democracy is that legitimate authority of any kind must rest on popular consent. Given how important authority exercised in the international system is becoming, the same test must be applied there too. Critical democratic theorists increasingly look to the international level as the crucial test for their ideas about democracy (Habermas, 2001; Scheuerman, 2006). Constructivism and critical theory are ultimately compatible because "Constructivism problematizes both agents and structures, it explores the dynamics of change as well as the rhythms of stasis, it calls into question established understandings of world politics, it is analytically open not closed. For these reasons it is necessarily 'critical' in the sense meant by Habermas" (Price and Reus-Smit, 1998: 288). Some constructivists have come to accept the possibility of dispersed and competent influence over the content and weight of discourses (Finnemore and

Sikkink, 2001: 400). And that kind of influence is one of the pillars of discursive democracy, involving critical engagement of discourses in the public sphere that produces public opinion, which in turn can influence collective decision-making (Dryzek, 2000).[8] In the hands of Habermas (1996) the public sphere in question is confined within national boundaries, and collective decision-making is carried out (in government textbook fashion) by the state. But public spheres can also be international in scope (see Cochran, 1999, 2002). They can be linked to the popular notion of transnational civil society, or global civil society, and indeed Thompson (1999) refers to a "civil societarian" approach to transnational democracy. However, discursive democracy can transcend civil society, which is just one home for sources of communicative power.[9] International public spheres can be composed of NGOs, individual activists, journalists, corporations, and members of governments and international governmental organizations acting in non-authoritative fashion. It is a particular kind of communication that defines public spheres – not a list of participants. Discursive democracy can be taken into the international system, which is exactly what I intend doing in subsequent chapters.

This approach to democracy rests on a tension between two related phenomena: first, the importance of discourses in ordering the world (and its conflicts); second, the potential for the structure of discourses to itself become the target of popular reflection and conscious action. The tension here arises because if discourses were readily manipulable by human agents then they would lack any independent ordering force of their own. But they are not manipulable at will. Human action takes place within the context that discourses provide: discourses themselves both enable and constrain actions.[10] Actions can draw on existing discourses, and so subtly affect the content and relative weight of discourses. To use the language of Bourdieu (1993), the structure of a discursive field constrains the positions that can be taken by actors but is itself reproduced by subsequent actions and interactions. Most actions simply reinforce the prevailing constellation of discourses. Walker (1993) argues that this includes the practice of academic international relations. But reflective action can sometimes bend it in different directions (especially in times of crisis). Wendt (1999: 375) argues that the states system is increasingly able to secure "critical self-reflection" in "the public sphere of international society, an emerging space where states appeal to public reason to hold each other accountable." There is no reason to restrict such capacity to states, and indeed every democratic reason to extend this capacity to a broad variety of actors and activists. Agents in the discursive realm can be arrayed in ways that reflect material inequalities: so wealthy and militarily strong actors such as states and corporations can sometimes exercise overwhelming influence over the terms of discourse. But agents can also be arrayed more democratically in the sense of a relatively dispersed and equal critical discursive capacity.

Democracy here cannot be interpreted in electoral terms, as universal suffrage for everyone affected by an international issue. Transnational discursive democracy does not have to be integrated with any particular set of formal institutions (though it can target influence over many such institutions, including states). Democracy is about communication as well as voting, about social learning as well as decision-making, and it is the communicative aspects that for the moment can most straightforwardly be pursued in the international system. This project is especially urgent in light of an international system whose dominant actors seem intent on rolling back democratic rights and freedoms in the name of global security.

Two other democratic projects are currently prominent on the global stage, and I will have more to say about both in the concluding chapter. The first is the neoconservative agenda of forcing states to become liberal democracies. However, neoconservatism is not interested in, is indeed hostile to, democracy above the level of the nation-state. The second project exists more in the realm of theory than practice. This is the model of cosmopolitan democracy, that seeks an international system more densely populated by formal institutions such as legislatures and courts that are directly accountable to the citizens of the world (rather than at one remove, through the democratic accountability of states that join international institutions). Cosmopolitans seek intermediate steps on the road to this ideal, involving, for example, a strengthened and more inclusive United Nations Security Council, an effective International Criminal Court, cross-national referenda, and a developing body of cosmopolitan international law. One of my goals in this book is to show that an approach to democracy emphasizing dispersed and competent control over the engagement of discourses in international public spheres is feasible and attractive. I will try to show that transnational discursive democracy can address *all* the conflicts I have outlined in this chapter, including the very hardest cases that a divided world presents: terrorism and counter-terror, the alleged clash of civilizations, and violent conflict in divided societies. In the final chapter I will explicitly compare transnational discursive democracy with neoconservative and cosmopolitan alternatives.

Two Kinds of Deliberative Global Politics

Deliberative global politics can be found in two sorts of places. The first consists of formal negotiations. These might take place in institutions such as the UN and its agencies, the EU, or the International Labor Organization; in multilateral negotiations of the kind that produced the WTO and Kyoto Protocol on greenhouse emissions; in diplomatic talks aimed at solving a particular problem or conflict; and in problem-solving forums involving states and other actors (styled "international discursive designs" in Dryzek, 1990: 77–108). For example, Risse (2000) analyzes the negotiations between the United States, the Soviet Union, NATO, and Germany over the reunification of Germany in 1989–90. He finds that key participants were open to argument and persuasion. This amenability to persuasion was especially true of Soviet leader Mikhail Gorbachev. Gorbachev was persuaded in the negotiations that a unified Germany within NATO redefined as a collective security organization as opposed to an anti-Soviet alliance would be better for European security than a unified Germany outside NATO – and much better than any of the obstructive options at his disposal (such as keeping Soviet troops on German soil, which the Soviet Union was legally entitled to do). The negotiations were in an important sense deliberative, though not especially democratic. For deliberation occurs whenever participants are amenable to changing their minds as a result of reflection induced by non-coercive communication. Deliberation only becomes deliberative *democracy* to the degree it provides opportunities for participation by all those affected by a decision.

Looking to high-level politics is consistent with one strand in deliberative theory that sees the proper home for deliberation in the formal institutions of the sovereign state, such as courts, legislatures, and policy-making committees (for example, Bessette, 1994; Rawls, 1997). Institutions of this sort are of course thin on the ground in the international system. And as the German reunification example suggests, even when peak policy-making processes do exist, it is much easier to find deliberation across leaders in these sorts of locations than it is to find deliberative *democracy*. For these reasons I will deploy instead a second strand in deliberative democratic theory, which looks to the potential for diffuse communication in the public sphere that generates public opinion that can in turn exercise political influence (Benhabib, 1996; Habermas, 1996; Dryzek, 2000). In its standard presentation in the context of national politics, that influence is exercised over the state. In applying the idea to international politics, influence can be exercised over international governmental organizations, the content of treaties and diplomatic negotiations, and the actions of states and corporations within the system. So, for example, human rights NGOs and activists may induce a particular oppressive state to change its ways by generating bad publicity, and convincing other states to withhold financial aid. Equally important to the exercise of influence on

27

authority is the fact that deliberation in the public sphere can also involve the reconstruction of relationships. This "social learning" aspect of deliberation can occur in the absence of any influence over formal decision-making (Kanra, 2005). In a divided world, deliberation as social learning is crucial when it comes to engagement across discourses as an alternative to violence between partisans. These sorts of conflicts across and within societies constitute some of the most severe and intractable problems in today's world, so with these I begin in the next chapter.

2

From the Clash of Civilizations to the Engagement of Discourses

One of the more prominent recent interpretations of world politics treats conflict in international affairs as mainly and increasingly a matter of the clash of civilizations. Originally proposed by Samuel Huntington in a 1993 article and 1996 book as a way to make sense of the post-Cold War world, the idea of such a clash gained further plausibility in 2001 with the attacks by Islamic radicals on the World Trade Center and Pentagon. These attacks and the responses to them seemed to signal intensification of a conflict between Islam and the West. Huntington himself sees the core issue in this conflict as Islam itself, not Islamic fundamentalism, on the grounds that an absolutist and universalist religion like Islam finds compromise and sharing space with other faiths and cultures very hard (Huntington, 1996: 217).

For Huntington, the world is divided up into at least eight civilizations: Western, Orthodox, Islamic, Latin American, African, Sinic (Chinese), Japanese, and Hindu. The set is not quite collectively exhaustive and mutually exclusive; Africa is only "possibly" a civilization (ibid.: 47), Latin America has some Western affinities, and Buddhism almost makes the list (ibid.: 47–8).

The differences between civilizations are presumably very old, so one question is why exactly should this clash now move to the forefront of international affairs? Part of Huntington's answer is the decline of the clash of ideologies that ordered so many conflicts during the Cold War. The other part is modernization, which Huntington is careful to distinguish from Westernization. Modernization involves technological change and increasing levels of literacy and education, intensifying interactions between civilizations. While other civilizations may adopt technologies and products developed in the West, they may simultaneously reject Western values. Huntington treats Western values – notably, individualism, separation of church and state, the rule of law, representative democracy and a respect for human rights – as culturally specific, not universal. The West's project should then be to defend these values in their home, not impose them on everybody else. I will argue that modernization can indeed facilitate the seeming clash of civilizations – but with an accent on the "seeming," so not in quite the way Huntington supposes. What Huntington ascribes to modernization is in fact a process of reflexive traditionalization (as described in chapter 1), in which increased awareness of competing traditions and their implications leads to defensive retreat into some version of one's own tradition. Yet this very act of retreat, and the awareness that causes it, themselves mean that one's own tradition becomes altered, radicalized, or perhaps even created anew. Those advocating such retreat draw very selectively on interpretations of the past and events therein – such as ancestral homelands, moments of glory, key defeats, unique suffering, and acts of betrayal. The discourses produced or modified by reflexive traditionalization can take on "civilizational" form, though ethnic nationalism, religious fundamentalism, and racism that do not necessarily coincide with civilizational entities are also possible (see chapter 3).

Much ink has been spilled by critics and defenders of the clash of civilizations thesis. I will not go through these familiar debates here. Instead, I will examine the alleged clash of civilizations through a discourse-analytic lens. I will justify treating "civilizations" as constructed by discourses, and interpret their appearance, conflict, and engagement in this light.

A Grim Future of Conflict?

The future according to Huntington is not one of productive and peaceful coexistence across civilizations, but rather one of hardening loyalties and potentially violent conflicts. "Emerging intercivilizational relations will normally vary from distant to violent" (1996: 207). The best that can be done is recognition of this grim reality, which can then be managed in balance-of-power terms in order to prevent violence getting too far beyond control. Core states should not intervene in the internal affairs of other civilizations (ibid.: 316), still less try to make states in other civilizations behave according to their own norms (so Huntington ought to oppose the neo-conservative project in the United States, which seeks to do exactly this in countries such as Iraq). Indeed, such intervention is Huntington's scenario for the outbreak of World War III, after the US intercedes on behalf of Vietnam against China. There are strong echoes here of the realist view of international relations, whose basic units were states (not civilizations) always poised at the edge of conflict (O'Hagan, 2000: 149). Realists believe that to survive in the anarchy which is the international system, states must always maximize their strategic position in relation to other states. They must do whatever is expedient in this cause, be it economic development, forming alliances, or going to war. Huntington wants to make civilizations more like states used to be (though he is careful to point out that civilizations do not do most of the things that states do; 1996: 44). He worries about civilizations that lack a core state (notably Islam and Africa) because then "fault line wars" at the boundaries of civilizations cannot easily be prevented or brought under control through imposition of solutions by core states on both sides. To help manage conflict, he proposes that each civilization should have a permanent seat on the United Nations Security Council.

This last proposal resembles a popular solution for the management of conflict in divided societies at the level of the state. The idea of "consociational democracy" was first outlined by Arend Lijphart in an interpretation of deeply divided societies that have managed to resolve their differences peacefully. Essentially, the model involves "grand coalition, segmental autonomy, proportionality, and minority veto" (Lijphart, 2000: 228), resulting from agreement across the various blocs to share power. But consociationalism is not especially democratic; it is a deal among elites that casts citizens in a passive role, no longer with any real say in determining who governs, because the composition of governments is not affected by election results. Citizens belonging to different blocs do not need to learn how to live with each other, because "segmental autonomy" means they will interact almost exclusively with fellow bloc members, be it in schools, universities, churches, voluntary associations, political parties, workplaces, or settlements. Lijphart claims successes for this model in his own Netherlands (with Catholic, Protestant, and secular blocs), several other small European countries, and even South Africa (in its transition from apartheid), India, and Canada.

Substitute "civilization" for "bloc" and the result is Huntington's blueprint for how civilizations ought to interact: through pacts negotiated by their elites that give each civilization segmental autonomy. Internally, civilizations consolidate their identity; while interactions across civilizational boundaries are kept to a minimum. No state should interfere in the internal affairs of another civilization. A permanent seat for each civilization in the United Nations Security Council is a form of minority veto. Obviously there is no global "state," so "grand coalition" is not at issue – but the idea is similar, to bring leadership from each civilization into a system of governance.

So how well has consociational government worked in divided societies at the level of the state? Outside a few small European countries (Netherlands, Belgium, Switzerland), the record is not too encouraging. At least one consociational regime, in Lebanon in the 1970s, has degenerated into civil war as a static division of power could not adjust to a changing balance of social forces. Consociational arrangements work by freezing cleavages, such that the establishment of such a regime may in practice simply reinforce or indeed even create the sort of inter-bloc conflict it is supposed to ameliorate or manage (Reynolds, 2000: 169–70). Thus the risk is that establishing such an arrangement at the international level would reinforce the very clash of civilizations it is supposed to solve. Construction of the solution means discursive construction or reinforcement of the problem. Such an arrangement would help lock the world into a future of conflicting camps whose hostilities are managed only by elites who have the good sense to control and minimize interactions between individuals from different civilizations. However, in Huntington's terms, the fact that elites come from different civilizations means that they will never trust each other, so the arrangement could only ever be a holding action against inter-civilizational violence, not a step on the road to reconciliation.

When it comes to the internal organization of civilizations, Huntington suggests in effect a process of "civilization-building" analogous to "state-building." State-building has substantial symbolic or discursive components, especially if elites need to establish or consolidate a national identity to accompany their claims to statehood. Civilization-building would have to be a still more thoroughly symbolic affair, given the lack of centralized coercive capacity on the part of civilizations (except where one state defines a civilization in Huntington's terms, as in Japan and India, and almost with China). The historical record shows that state-building that deploys a symbolic politics of identity can be a very bloody affair. State-building elites often try to engineer a collective identity to bolster their own power. The result is bad news for those defined as the "other" in order to consolidate this identity, be they Jews in fifteenth-century Spain, Huguenots in seventeenth-century France, Armenians in early twentieth-century Turkey, or Bosnians in 1990s Yugoslavia (see Rae, 2002). Huntington surely does not intend to provide license to civilization-building elites to engage in the genocide that has historically accompanied the efforts of state-building elites to homogenize their populations. But clearly it is a danger that accompanies his suggestions. To explore how matters might play out differently, we can reconstruct the alleged clash of civilizations in discourse-analytic terms.

Identity is a Creation of Discourse, Not Culture

Huntington defines civilizations in terms of the cultures and identities at their core. "A civilization is a culture writ large" (1996: 41). "A Civilization is . . . the broadest level of cultural identity people have short of what distinguishes humans from other species" (ibid.: 43). In sliding between culture and identity, Huntington is implicitly assuming that identities are the product of cultures: that who I think I am is determined by the culture I belong to. But a culture is not the same as an identity. A culture is a shared set of ingrained practices and dispositions, while an identity is a conception of who I am and who I am not. A culture and its aspects can be taken for granted, an identity has to be a matter of conscious awareness. It is possible for individuals to share a culture and have different identities. For example, different individuals in Russia may share Russian culture, but identify variously as Russian nationalists, citizens of Europe, communists nostalgic for the Soviet era, localists at loggerheads with Moscow, or none of the above. Some might even conceivably identify with a larger Orthodox civilization.

Huntington's slippage between culture and identity here mirrors that of the multiculturalists he otherwise opposes so vehemently. The core premise of multicultural liberals such as Kymlicka (1995) is that identities are generated by cultures. Multiculturalists therefore believe that identity conflicts can be solved by validating the claims of minority subcultures and protecting them in a legal and political order. Appropriate measures might include autonomy for regions populated by minority cultures, legal recognition and promotion of minority languages, and parliamentary quotas. Huntington himself would have none of this, for he believes that multiculturalism is a serious threat to core Western values. In his 2004 book *Who Are We?*, Huntington identifies the main threat to the United States as Latin American immigration that dilutes the country's protestant character. But he shares the basic idea that identities and the conflicts they engender are a product of culture.

Identity, including civilizational identity of the sort Huntington highlights, is not necessarily or even mainly a matter of culture. As Moore (1999) points out, societies such as Northern Ireland and Rwanda that are deeply divided when it comes to identity are often hardly divided at all when it comes to culture, and this is often recognized by the different sides. Conversely, culturally divided societies such as Switzerland do not necessarily exhibit identity differences. Culturally, there is very little difference between (for example) Croats, Serbs, and Muslims in the former Yugoslavia, even though they can be located in three of Huntington's civilizations (respectively, Western, Orthodox, and Islamic). Bosnia was home to one of the world's most secular Muslim communities. These three communities went to war in the 1990s not as the most recent act in a bloody inter-civilizational play, but because it was in the interests of political leaders to invoke national identity conflicts in order to consolidate their own power and hold over their own populations. Even then, there was initially substantial resistance among Bosnian Muslims to casting their resistance in sectarian terms – as opposed to the terms of secular modernity besieged by ethnic nationalism. Here and elsewhere, ethnic hatreds are the product mostly of symbolic politics engaged by both leaders and masses (Kaufman, 2001); they are not just some primordial legacy. Ethnic identities such as "Croat" and "Serb" are the product of the twentieth century, prior to which most identities were probably local (ibid.: 4–5).

Nations, as Benedict Anderson (1983) points out, are "imagined communities"; they need to be mobilized into existence through symbols invoked by political leadership. As such, they are the products of discourses. The same might be said for civilizations, which have no essential cultural existence prior to their mobilization by discursive means. Bosnian Muslims, Saudis, and most Indonesians belong to the same civilization in Huntington's terms. But culturally, Bosnian Muslims resemble Serbs more than they resemble Indonesians; and in their comparatively relaxed attitudes to religion, both Indonesians and Bosnians have little in common culturally with Saudis. Samuel Huntington and Osama bin Laden alike would, however, want to herd them into a common civilizational identity.

Once established, national identities can be extraordinarily persistent, even in the face of cultural change (Moore, 1999: 38). Those subscribing to a national identity are normally only satisfied if they have a state to go along with it – or at least some formal recognition of that aspiration. Demobilizing an established national identity is extraordinarily hard. Thus anyone advocating, as Huntington does, the mobilization of civilizational identity in terms that are national identity writ large ought to think long and hard about what they are doing, because the consequences could be irreversible.

In some, perhaps most, of Huntington's cases, mobilization into an imagined community encompassing the civilization has not actually occurred. Huntington himself attempts discursive mobilization of "the West"; within Islam there are those engaged in mobilization too. Most other civilizations do not see civilizational mobilization on such a scale, if at all. It is almost absent in Latin America and Africa. India saw Hindu nationalism advance in the 1990s, but by 2004 Hindu Nationalist Prime Minister Vajpayee Rao was appealing for votes from India's Muslims (his party still lost that year's general election).

Civilizational identities do then have to be mobilized; they are not just "there," or automatically generated by culture. So is there something about today's world conducive to such mobilization along civilizational lines? I will now answer this question in the affirmative, though the answer is different from Huntington's own, and so the clashes that such mobilizations produce may yield to treatments very different from those he prescribes.

Modernization
and the Discursive Mobilization of Clashes

Some of the discourses that have attained prominence since the relative simplicity once provided by the Cold War can indeed be captured plausibly in civilizational terms, and actors such as Slobodan Milosevic, Samuel Huntington, Osama bin Laden, and Lee Kwan Yew have tried to advance their claims. And when such "civilizational" discourses do come to the fore it is often in terms of a clash, because any such discourse needs a constitutive other or others by which to define itself. So Milosevic defines Serb nationalism in terms of struggles against both "the Turk" and (Western) Croatian fascism. Huntington promotes "Atlanticism" (1996: 312) against Islam, East Asia, and multiculturalists at home. Osama bin Laden wants to mobilize Islam against the West (and to a lesser degree against the Orthodox world). Lee Kwan Yew defines Asian values of community and hierarchy against a decadent and individualistic West. Though cast in civilizational terms, the case of Lee Kwan Yew does not actually fit Huntington's categories, because the Asian values discourse extends across Sinic, Japanese, Islamic, and possibly Hindu "civilizations."

Certainly, discourses capable of being described in civilizational terms can now be found in the international system, often to profound effect. But discourses that cannot be described in civilizational terms can also be found in the international system, to equally profound effect. Discourses that are not civilization-specific include globalization, anti-corporate globalization, sustainable development, anarchy (as understood by realist practitioners of international relations), market liberalism, counter-terror, and democracy. Such discourses may of course be more pervasive in some parts of the world than others, and some of them are tied by their opponents to particular civilizations. So, for example, Lee Kwan Yew would see the rights discourse as essentially Western (but happily accept globalization as universal). The leadership of the Chinese Communist Party might say the same about democracy. But none of these discourses specifies civilization-specific attributes as part of its core ontology. The fact that a discourse may play out differently in different places is no argument for its civilizational specificity.

In short, the international system is home to constellations of discourses, some but not all of which can be described in civilizational terms. There are plenty of other options. Sometimes discourses clash, and sometimes that clash can be interpreted in civilizational terms.

Sometimes the contest is more ambiguous. For example, in the wake of the 1997 East Asian financial crisis, the kind of cooperative capitalism that had seemed so successful in producing economic growth in the region now came under attack from market liberalism, as advanced by the International Monetary Fund in particular. The IMF is headquartered in Washington, was set up at Bretton Woods after World War II as part of a system designed by the United States, and adopted market liberalism in the early 1980s under influence from the Reagan administration. So were the post-crisis negotiations and upheavals a clash between the West and Asian civilizations? Or simply between two variants of capitalism? The cooperative variant is not unique to the Sinic, Islamic, and Japanese countries of East Asia; it applies to a degree in corporatist West European countries. And the wrath of the IMF is applied to countries in the "Western" category too (such as the Philippines). The market liberal discourse to which the IMF subscribes is itself contested within the West (Stiglitz, 2002). So to treat the fallout from the East Asian financial crisis in terms of a clash of civilizations would be at best a gross oversimplification.

There is indeed a kernel of plausibility in the clash of civilizations thesis, which should not be dismissed out of hand. Modernization can be accompanied by reflexive traditionalization, and so does appear to facilitate the clash of civilizations – but that clash is actually just one manifestation of broader processes involving the erosion of hegemonic discourses in the international system described in chapter 1.

Some of these emerging processes can ameliorate rather than exacerbate inter-civilizational contests.

Huntington's analysis of modernization and its effects turns out to miss two important features. In this section I have emphasized the first, the degree to which the communication and reflection accompanying modernization create space for non-civilizational discourses. A second important feature, to which I now turn, is the degree to which modernization facilitates contestation within as well as across civilizational discourses. Such contestation can be accompanied by dialogue and reflection, not just the kind of dogmatism and rejection of the other stressed by Huntington.

Reflection and Contestation within "Civilizations"

Criticism, resistance, and reflection can occur within as well as across the boundaries of "civilizations." Inasmuch as he treats civilizational identities as given (rather than discursively created), Huntington is denying the possibility of internal reflection and contestation. The main process at work for him would be socialization, which by definition is mostly unreflective. In these terms, one is, for example, raised a Hindu or Chinese, and part of that is acquiring a civilizational identity. There is, oddly, an affinity here between the conservative Huntington and the radical Michel Foucault, who relates the history of discourses primarily in terms of their encompassing and (for Foucault) mostly oppressive character. It is discourses that create identities (though Huntington would here speak in terms of cultures rather than discourses). For both Huntington and Foucault, reflective choice across cultures or discourses is likely to be both rare and problematic.

But once we accept that identities are not given by cultures, this kind of analysis appears too one-dimensional and deterministic. The mobilization of identity does not of course proceed from scratch; and it may find resources in a particular culture or subculture for its appeals. But those appeals can also be contested by others drawing on the same culture – or indeed upon aspects of other cultures. "Civilizations" are not the monoliths that Huntington portrays (or wants them to be), unchanging in their essential character.

Contestation certainly exists within Huntington's own Western civilization. Huntington himself bemoans the rise of multiculturalism in the United States as a weakening of the "American creed," a Trojan horse for non-Western values. But the very fact that Huntington feels the need to argue against multiculturalism shows that some in the West are arguing for it; that there is an identity contest under way concerning the future of the West. Moreover, the multiculturalists them-selves can find resources in Western political traditions for their arguments – notably, ideals of human rights, the recogni-tion of different others which these ideals imply, and individual fulfillment that needs to be grounded in cultural group membership (Kymlicka, 1995). Another kind of con-testation was very evident within the West prior to the invasion of Iraq by US and British forces in 2003, with the governments and peoples of France and Germany advocating an attitude to the Islamic world at variance with the belliger-ence of British and American governments. This difference put an end to Huntington's earlier claim that "European gov-ernments and publics have largely supported and rarely criticized actions the United States has taken against its Muslim opponents" (1996, p. 217).

But are such internal contests confined to the West? Is there something unique about the West that makes such internal contest possible, while it is not possible in other civi-lizations? Or could it be that it is the forces of modernization that make such internal contests more likely? If the latter case holds, then, on Huntington's own account, these contests ought also to become more likely in other civilizations. Hunt-ington recognizes such conflicts, but treats them as problems that need to be overcome – and he implies the only solution is for a society to find its proper civilization home. Turkey, for example, is treated as a case of a "torn" country, whose elites look to the West while its people look to Islam (1996: 144–9).

Huntington believes that democracy and modernization will lead to increasing Islamization of Turkish politics; but as of 2005, even the main Islamist parties want to join the European Union. Another interpretation of Turkish politics is that the contest between Islamic and secular forces goes all the way down from elites to masses; its secular discourse of Kemalism (following Mustafa Kemal Ataturk, founder of the modern Turkish state) is not just the preserve of elites. Iran's development of a fundamentalist form of political Islam after the 1979 revolution eventually became internally contested, and those styled modernizers in Iran do among other things seek a less confrontational outlook toward the West, as well as greater flexibility in enforcing religious dogma at home. As Benhabib (2002) argues at length, cultures that are in Huntington's terms "civilizational" may look monolithic on a cursory view from the outside, but closer inspection shows that they are internally polyvocal.

Modernization is accompanied by improved educational levels, literacy, communications, and so awareness of alternative identities and ways of life. Huntington asserts that awareness will normally lead to rejection of these alternatives, what can be described as reflexive traditionalization, but other outcomes are on the face of it just as likely. Huntington explains the invigoration of anti-Western identities in terms of reaction against Westernization, a reaction which is itself facilitated by modernization. What this suggests is that modernization increases the capacity for reflective choice. But he provides no mechanism as to why reflection will normally confirm and intensify one's civilizational identity; that is, why it has to end in traditionalization.

Engagements Across Boundaries

Huntington's approach to the management of civilizational conflict is to treat civilizations as properly homogenous, unitary entities whose interactions ought to be controlled by elites in top-down fashion. Sensitivity to the discursive constitution of international affairs immediately suggests that any actions taken along such lines are likely to reinforce the intensity of inter-civilizational hostility, as I pointed out earlier. The alternative is a "bottom-up" approach that treats any clash as subject to amelioration by the engagement of discourses, which may or may not be defined on a civilizational basis.

For cultures are not seamless wholes, nor are identities, nor are civilizations. The idea that cultures are unitary entities is an error shared by contemporary multiculturalists and "clash" conservatives. But many of the features that outsiders attribute to a particular culture, and even see as defining the culture, are often hotly contested within it (Benhabib, 2002). And this contestation opens possibilities for dialogue across boundaries. Consider for example the question of female genital cutting, a cultural practice often thought central in the parts of Africa where (in Huntington's terms) African and Islamic civilizations meet, and one regarded with horror by most Westerners (except for academic cultural relativists). There are groups within these societies that are trying to end the practice; the key is simply to get families to agree formally in a public contract that they will regard young women who have not been mutilated as eligible for marriage. Such public contracts prove remarkably swift and comprehensive in changing allegedly ingrained cultural practices, as Mackie (1996) points out.

One inter-civilizational approach to this issue involves condemnation of female genital cutting as either a violation of universal human rights or as an extreme manifestation of patriarchy. Approaches of this sort are likely only to raise the stakes and help make the practice a marker of identity, so generating resistance to its abolition. A more productive approach to engagement would start from an understanding of the particular situation of the women involved, and the way they perceive their own needs. Mackie's "convention" account of how women can organize abandonment of the practice is a piece of soft rational choice analysis developed in the West that proves to shed light on how a practice might be changed. This analysis is also consistent with communal abandonment ceremonies that have been organized by women in countries such as Senegal. The general point here is that dialogue across alleged civilizational boundaries can be productive to the extent it focuses on the particular needs of individuals and groups, as opposed to general principles and markers of identity. To the degree head-on confrontation between competing principles is avoided, the other side can less easily be charged with attempting covertly to seek political domination, and one's own side can less readily argue that it is in a desperate struggle to safeguard its religion, culture, identity, or civilization.

This sort of discursive engagement across deep differences in identity can be difficult within state boundaries because sovereignty is at issue. Under the principles solidified in the wake of the Peace of Westphalia in 1648, sovereignty has had an all or nothing character to it; one either has a sovereign entity to accompany one's identity, or one has nothing. But in interactions within the international system itself, sovereignty over the system as a whole is not an issue (unless one's faith is truly absolutist, in the sense that one believes that everyone in the world should follow it). And for the moment, nothing like sovereignty is currently at issue at the civilizational level – though Huntington would like to change that (as would Osama bin Laden, who dreams of re-establishing the Caliphate). Thus one can at least imagine transnational engagement of discourses proceeding according to norms of civility that are much harder to achieve in the context of an all-or-nothing sovereignty contest over a particular piece of territory. When particular oppressed groups take their struggle into the international system, they have to abide by the norms of transnational civil society in order to garner cross-civilizational support. Some groups have been especially successful in gaining this sort of attention, notably the Zapatistas in Mexico and the Ogoni in Nigeria. Such groups have been exemplary in their adherence to discursive norms of transnational interaction. These norms are not Western impositions. Instead, they are standards that emerge out of the interactions of individuals and groups from different "civilizations."[1]

Bottom-up approaches to cross-"civilizational" engagement and dialogue cannot be a complete substitute for top-down conflict management in the international system. But we should beware of establishing and consolidating top-down mechanisms that make engagement and dialogue more difficult. Huntington's proposed internal homogenization of civilizations, hardening of their boundaries, and validation of their global standing would have exactly this effect. Top-down conflict management can also be conducted by states, not civilizations, or "core states" acting on behalf of civilizations. While the history of conflict management by states is not exactly salutary, assigning the task to civilizational entities is likely only to make matters worse by raising the stakes in conflicts and constituting discursive reinforcement of the idea that the world is indeed defined by its mutually hostile civilizations.

Conclusion

The widespread attention commanded by the clash of civilizations thesis suggests it has plenty of resonance in world affairs. The plausibility of the thesis can be explained by treating the appearance of discourses seemingly defined on a civilizational basis as just one manifestation of the degree to which international conflicts now feature contending discourses, rather than states or alliances confronting one another. But their interaction does not have to take the form of hostility that needs to be managed and so reinforced in top-down fashion. Instead, it can feature deliberative engagement in transnational public spheres. I will address this possibility at greater length at the end of the next chapter, which looks at how murderous identity conflicts can take shape in particular divided societies, the most graphic manifestations of the alleged clash of civilizations. I will look at what can be done to resolve these conflicts in deliberative and democratic fashion.

3

Deliberation
in Divided Societies

The politics of identity underlies many divisions in today's world. Some of these identities are "civilizational" but many are not. All seek validation in opposition to the identity of some other category of people. Sometimes this opposition is expressed in reasonably peaceful terms, and processed through conventional political channels. At other times opposition becomes violent, expressed in warfare that constitutes some of the major stresses in the contemporary international system.

Once wars were fought between states or groups of states. But what Mary Kaldor (1999) calls "new wars" are much more common in today's divided world. As Kaldor points out, new wars are fought between networks that might be composed of guerrillas, warlords, mercenaries, terrorists, criminals, regular military forces that owe allegiance to some government somewhere, and diasporas of supporters.[1] Conflict itself involves attacks on civilians as much as battle between military forces, taking place in a variety of locations but centered on territory where no state can successfully establish any claim to sovereign authority – and, in particular, an effective monopoly of legitimate use of coercion, which is normally taken as the key attribute of effective state authority. New wars have proliferated since the end of the Cold War; examples may be found in the former Yugoslavia, the Caucasus, and Africa. New wars generally involve a clash of groups sub-scribing to identities that appear to require denial of the identity of the other side. Sometimes they can be interpreted in terms of Huntington's "clash of civilizations," as when representatives of Western, Islamic, and Orthodox civilizations fight in former Yugoslavia, or when Islamic Chechens battle Orthodox Russians. But they can also occur within alleged civilizational blocs; this is especially true in Africa, but has also characterized Northern Ireland.

These sorts of wars are the more violent manifestations of divided societies. A divided society is defined by mutually contradictory assertions of identity. The assertions in question might involve nationalism (Republicans and Unionists in Northern Ireland, any number of separatist movements), combinations of religious and ethnic conflicts (Palestinians versus Israelis), religious versus secular forces (Islamic funda-mentalism against Western liberalism on the global stage; Islamists versus secularists in Turkey and Algeria; Christian fundamentalists versus liberalism in the United States). The basic problem in all these cases is that one identity can only be validated or, worse, constituted by suppression of another. Radical Islamists cannot live in or with what Benjamin Barber (1995) called "McWorld." A state that was no longer a Jewish state forged in struggle would be anathema to many Israelis. Christian fundamentalists regard the political presence of gays and lesbians not just as an irritant, but as a standing affront to who they are. A multinational society is not just a policy opposed by militant Serb nationalists, it is a perceived attack on their core political being. These sorts of conflicts lie at the heart of some of the toughest political issues in the con-temporary world. Identity politics, including the murderous variety, are hardly new. But as the Cold War world order fell apart, the political gap was often filled by assertions and denials of identity. Religious fundamentalisms showed renewed vigor, in opposition to each other as well as "McWorld."

In this chapter I shall argue that even severe clashes of identity can be countered by democratic means. Indeed, democracy can speak much more readily to these clashes of identity than it can to clashes between states of the sort that produced "old wars."[2] The means in question are located in the deliberative or communicative aspects of democracy. On the face of it, deliberation across divided identities ought to be hard. For on a widely shared account, deliberation is what Bessette (1994) calls the "mild voice of reason" – exactly what is lacking in tough identity issues, at best an aspiration for how opponents might one day learn to interact once their real differences are dissolved. Deliberative democrats influenced by John Rawls (1993) might follow him in excluding the "background culture" from the purview of deliberation that involves only public reason – that is, reasoning in impartial terms about the political arrangements that are best for society as a whole. Gutmann and Thompson (1996) believe that deliberation can be extended to deep *moral* disagreements, but the precondition is commitment on all sides to reciprocity, "the capacity to seek fair terms of cooperation for its own sake," such that arguments are made in terms the other side(s) can accept. Again, mutual acceptance of reasonableness is exactly what is lacking in divided societies. Gutmann and Thompson require adoption by all sides of a particular moral psychology – openness to persuasion by critical argument – that is in fact not widely held, and explicitly rejected by (say) fundamentalist Christians (Fish, 1999: 92–3). Those asserting identities may feel insulted by the very idea that questions going to their core be deliberated. What they want is instead "cathartic" communication that unifies the group and demands respect from others (Simon, 1999: 50–2).

I argue for a discursive democracy that can handle deep differences. The key involves partially decoupling the deliberation and decision aspects of democracy, locating deliberation in engagement of discourses in the public sphere at a distance from any contest for sovereign authority. The public spheres in question can transcend national boundaries, and their transnational aspects can have an important moderating influence on the clash of identities. I approach this argument by examining two very different responses to the challenge of divided societies. The first is agonistic, seeking robust and passionate exchange across identities. I focus on the work of Chantal Mouffe, because she explicitly advocates agonism against deliberative democracy in plural societies.[3] The second response is consociational, seeking suppression of interchange through agreement among well-meaning elites from different sides in a conflict. I will not treat these two as "straw man" extremes between which a moderate path should be sought. Indeed, I argue that a defensible discursive democracy for divided societies can develop elements of both.

Agonism

Agonists believe that deliberative democracy is incapable of processing deep difference. Mouffe (1999, 2000a, 2000b) argues that the main task for democracy is to convert antagonism into agonism, enemies into adversaries, fighting into critical engagement. Deep difference is accompanied by passions which, she believes, cannot be resolved by deliberation, committed as it is to rationalistic denial of passion and the pursuit of consensus that in practice both masks and serves power. Her alternative is agonistic pluralism involving "a vibrant clash of democratic political positions" (2000b: 16). "The prime task of democratic politics is not to eliminate the passions ... but to mobilise these passions towards the promotion of democratic designs" (1999: 755–6). Acceptance of the legitimacy of the positions of others comes not through being persuaded by argument, but through openness to conversion as a result of a particular kind of democratic attitude (ibid.: 755). The outcome is not agreement, but rather relationships that combine continued contestation with deep respect for the adversary – indeed it is not easy to speak in terms of "outcomes," because interaction is ongoing. Mouffe is vulnerable to questions about where exactly the required attitude should come from, especially where groups asserting identity themselves feature hierarchy and repression of their own members (Kapoor, 2002: 472–3).

While accepting Mouffe's identification of the need to transform antagonism into, if not agonism, at least more civilized engagement as the primary task for democracy in divided societies, I differ from her on three grounds. The first is in the content of critical interchange. Mouffe wants this interchange to be energized by core identities, otherwise passion is missing. Yet, paradoxically, identities for Mouffe have to be fluid to the extent of enabling thorough conversion in one group's attitude to another. But if identities themselves are highlighted, exchange is more likely to freeze identities than convert them. As Forester (1999b: 470–2) points out, being respectful of others is one thing; accepting at face value claims that preferences and interests are in fact basic values is quite another, requiring a more challenging order of problem-solving. If interchange is to move beyond confrontation and stalemate, then, Forester argues, the focus should be on the specific needs of the parties, not on the articulation and scrutiny of general value systems. His example concerns gay activists and fundamentalist Christians meeting over HIV/AIDS care in Colorado. The last thing that needs to be done is to reinforce mutually hostile identities, for example by debating whether or not it is legitimate to treat the HIV/AIDS issue in the moral terms favored by the Christians, as opposed to the public health terms favored by the gays. But if individuals can listen to each others' stories, they might at least accept one another's specific needs – which can be reconciled, even when value systems and identities cannot. This is a kind of reciprocal recognition, but not the kind of vibrant exchange of passions proposed by Mouffe.

A second departure from Mouffe involves the way deliberative interaction is conceptualized. Mouffe may be right that deliberation in the image of a philosophy seminar – dispassionate and reasoned – cannot handle deep difference. However, it is possible to formulate an account of discursive democracy that is more contestatory than this image, so more robust in the face of deep difference.

Third, Mouffe's interpretation of the main task of democracy has no obvious place for collective decision-making and resolution of social problems. She scorns consensus as a cover for power, but at least consensus implies that decisions can get made. When agonistic pluralism does attend to collective decisions, it is only to point to the need for them to be open to further contestation. I will explore a way to combine critical engagement and collective decision, but this will require a differentiation of the ways politics can be conducted in different sites. While Mouffe emphasizes the variety of sites (culture, workplace, home, school, etc.), for her the content of politics is undifferentiated, everywhere agonistic.

Consociational Democracy

A very different sort of criticism of deliberative democracy's ability to process divisive issues follows from arguments that they should be removed from contentious democratic debate altogether. From this perspective, Mouffe's (2000b: 16) assertion that "a well functioning democracy calls for a vibrant clash of democratic political positions" is naive, for "vibrant clashes" risk disintegration. Such is the basis of Arend Lijphart's (1977) claims for consociational democracy, an agreement between the leaders of each bloc to share government, involving "grand coalition, segmental autonomy, proportionality, and minority veto" (Lijphart, 2000: 228). Lijphart (1994: 222) believes consociationalism is "the only workable type of democracy in deeply divided societies." Lijphart claims successes in divided societies around the world, beginning with European cases such at the Netherlands, Austria, and Switzerland – which managed their conflicts so successfully that they are now seen as models of stability, their deep divisions long forgotten. With a bit more stretching, Lijphart identifies consociational elements in countries such as Malaysia, South Africa (at least in the 1994–6 dismantling of apartheid), and India. As we saw in chapter 2, Huntington's proposed solution for management of the clash of civilizations at the international level resembles this sort of arrangement – an elite pact to control conflictual populations by keeping them apart.

Despite its name, consociational democracy is not very democratic: elections make no difference to who is in power, as the same set of leaders governs irrespective of election results. Contentious deliberation is allowed only between the leaders of different blocs, and even then mostly in secret (for fear of inflaming publics), ruling out much of a role for parliamentary debate. The political communication of ordinary people is shepherded into within-bloc channels, where it can do little damage. This channeling obstructs any kind of deliberative, still less agonistic, interaction across different blocs below the elite level, because "segmental autonomy" is basic. Yet segmental autonomy is itself hazardous. As Reynolds (2000: 169–70) points out, it involves freezing existing cleavages into place. In so doing, conflict is perpetuated. And if the state does ever disintegrate, there are few defenses against the kind of mobilization that demagogues can undertake to convince people of the evil character of the other side, and the need to hate.

Consociation precludes any role that public deliberation construed as social learning might play in reconciliation in divided societies. A deliberative democrat would hope that reflection stimulated by interaction could contribute to less vicious symbolic politics, not tied to myths of victimhood and destiny. Segmental autonomy precludes such a politics, because deliberation confined within segments succumbs to Sunstein's (2002) "law of group polarization." Debate leads only to the group position becoming more extreme, as individuals get their prejudices confirmed in talk with like-minded others.

Toward a Deliberative Response

Agonists believe deliberative democracy cannot deal with divisive issues because it is too constraining in the kind of communication it allows. Consociationalists believe deliberative

51

democracy cannot deal with divisive issues because it is too open to diverse claims and claimants. Deliberative democracy can be defended against both sides, but it has to take them seriously, and be prepared to take elements from each. On the face of it, this ought to be impossible, given their diametric opposition. The key is a differentiation of political sites within a society which agonists and consociationalists alike have not contemplated: the former because they address only politics in the abstract rather than its institutional specifics, the latter because they see only a politics tightly attached to the sovereign state. Deliberative democracy can process contentious issues in a politics of engagement in the public sphere.

In this light, a conception of discursive democracy in terms of public spheres home to constellations of discourses can be brought to bear. As I have argued from the outset, discourses are amenable to reflection and reconstruction, if only at the margins. The associated communication is deliberation not agonism because it is oriented to persuasion rather than conversion, and retains some connection (however loose) to collective decision.

Agonists see deliberation as deadening and biased in the kind of communication it allows. But the engagement of discourses can accommodate many kinds of communication beyond reasoned argument, including rhetoric, testimony, performance, gossip, and jokes. However, three tests must be applied to secure the intersubjective understanding prized by deliberative democrats. Once we move beyond ritualistic openings, communication is required to be, first, capable of inducing reflection, second, non-coercive, and, third, capable of linking the particular experience of an individual or group with some more general point or principle (Dryzek, 2000, p. 68).[4] The last of these three criteria is crucial when it comes to identity politics gone bad. A harrowing story of (say) rape and murder in a Bosnian village can be told in terms of guilt of one ethnic group and violated innocence of another – fuel for revenge. But the story can also be told in terms of violation of basic principles of humanity which apply to all ethnicities, making reconciliation at least conceivable (though not easy).

Deliberation in Divided Societies

How can this discursive approach be applied to divided societies? To begin, we need to get beyond the idea that it is cultural differences that need to be reconciled. As Moore (1999) argues, the problem of divided societies is not one of cultural division. Different sides in divided societies can be culturally almost identical, as is the case with Catholics and Protestants in Northern Ireland. The same was true in Bosnia, with Serbs, Croats, and very secular Muslims exhibiting little cultural difference. The erroneous treatment of identity in terms of culture extends even to Benhabib's (2002) defense of universalist deliberative democracy against cultural relativism. She accepts that "culture has become a ubiquitous synonym for identity, an identity marker and differentiator" (p. 1), even as she "pleads for recognition of the radical hybridity and polyvocality of all cultures" (p. 25) that facilitates deliberation both within and across groups.

So how does violent conflict in divided societies arise, if it is not a matter of cultural differences, still less "primordial" communal hatreds? The answer is that identities can be mobilized by particular discourses, which in turn can be manipulated by demagogues. As Benedict Anderson (1983) points out, nations themselves are "imagined communities." They are produced by discourses, not by culture, and certainly not by genes. And if discourses underlie the problem, they can also underlie the solution. But how can reflective engagement across discourses move beyond the vain hopes of agonists when identities are only asserted dogmatically against each other, fueled by all kinds of resentments (as lamented by Connolly, 1991)?

Engagement is less likely to end in hostility if the focus is on specific needs (e.g., security, education) rather than general values. An example comes from Turkey, where headscarves worn by young Islamic women were long a symbolic marker that excluded them from secular Turkish universities. Beginning in 2002, a reframing of the issue in terms of the education needs of young women and the character of education as a basic human right gained ground, and the issue looked less intractable (Kanra, 2005). Avoidance of head-on confrontation means the other side is less easily accused of a hidden agenda to capture the state, and one's own side cannot so easily claim alone to represent "the people" or safeguard the polity (see the guidelines proposed by Fennema and Maussen, 2000).

A problem in emphasizing needs is that some needs can be manipulated to justify hostility. Notably, advocates of ethnic cleansing in former Yugoslavia argued that it was necessary to ensure the basic need of security, at least for their own side. But such arguments could resonate only within their own ethnic group. Demagogues can manipulate needs-talk in a destructive direction, just as they can manipulate any other kind of talk. A focus on needs is likely to contribute to conflict resolution only in the context of an engaged dialogue across difference, but not when communication is segmented within groups.

Deliberative rituals and indirect communication (as opposed to confrontation) also have roles to play in reconstructing relationships. Forester (1999a: 115–53) demonstrates the importance of (say) small talk between erstwhile opponents over a shared meal with no explicit connection to the issue at hand. Experiments show that even a period of irrelevant discussion can increase the incidence of subsequent cooperative behavior in individual decision-making (Orbell et al., 1988). So even cheap talk can help moderate conflict, though by itself such talk is insufficient to produce the requisite engagement across discourses.

Democracy and Formal Authority in Divided Societies

I turn now from the "what" to the "where" of deliberation, beginning by pointing to the desirability of loosening the connection between the deliberation and decision moments of democracy in a divided society. Such loosening resists one strong current in deliberative democratic theory, which sees the proper home for deliberation in the institutions of formal government, such as assemblies, legislatures, courts, public inquiries, committees, and administrative tribunals. To see why a degree of separation is desirable, consider what happens when deliberation and decision are joined in the context of divisive identity.

Mainly, decision overwhelms deliberation – especially when decision is tied to the construction of sovereign authority. Since the peace of Westphalia in 1648, sovereignty has been absolute, a matter of all or nothing when it comes to identity. Westphalia established the norm of non-interference in internal affairs (however much that norm has since been violated in practice), and the principle that the religion of the prince is the religion of the state. At the time in Europe, religion was the main, almost sole, identity that mattered. Later, identity came also to involve nationality, ethnicity, and class; but the idea of one identity per state persisted. Identity issues could become intractable in the context of the politics of the state: the game is all or nothing, a group either achieves a state that it can control or is subordinated by a state dominated by another group.

The very worst repression of competing identities has often come from actors struggling to secure their hold over a state, and the state's hold over a society. As Rae (2002) demonstrates, episodes ranging from expulsion and forced conversion of Jews in fifteenth-century Spain to the Armenian genocide in Turkey to ethnic cleansing in former Yugoslavia in the 1990s can all be attributed to state-building elites. These elites pursue what she calls "pathological homogenization" to secure a mass identity to accompany and bolster the incipient state. In the seventeenth century Thomas Hobbes argued that the "leviathan" of an absolutist sovereign was required to bring conflicting groups under control. The historical record shows in contrast that it is leviathan under construction that creates murder and misery, rather than curbing them.

Electoral democracy does not solve matters, and may exacerbate them. The game becomes one of insuring that the state is defined to be certain that one's favored identity will win key votes. This definition can involve drawing physical

boundaries, or manipulation of the electoral system, or gerry-
mandering, or suffrage restrictions (for example, measures
taken to stop African-Americans voting in the American
South, ranging over property qualifications, literacy tests, and
exclusion of those with a criminal record).

Multicultural liberals (for example, Kymlicka, 1995) have
addressed what a multi–identity state might look like –
though they err by treating identity differences as mere
cultural differences. Such a state might involve devolution of
authority to regions dominated by minority cultures, legal
recognition and promotion of minority languages, and group
representation (for example, parliamentary quotas for a particular group). These theorists are more compelling on the
liberal aspects of such a state – the specification of rights for
individuals and groups. They are less compelling when it
comes to the democratic aspects – how decisions should be
responsive to minority wishes. Proposals for group representation are fraught with difficulty when it comes to specifying
which groups count and how much representation they
have. If there is advantage in being categorized as an
oppressed minority, everyone will try to claim that status, so
raising divisions.[5]

How might deliberative democrats respond to the challenge posed by a deadly numbers game that can accompany
electoral politics? At one level they could pin their hopes on
the civilizing force of deliberation itself to defuse conflict. But
now the familiar scale problem arises: deliberation, at least of
the face-to-face variety connected tightly to state authority,
can only ever be for the few. Perhaps there are a few representatives who might be so civilized; but in a politics of mass
voting tightly connected to definition of the sovereign state,
they can all too easily be overwhelmed by demagogues. Thus
in Northern Ireland, the Democratic Unionist Party and Sinn
Fein still prosper at the expense of, respectively, the more
moderate "Official" Unionists and Social Democratic Labour
Party – even at a time when compromise is in the Northern
Irish air as never before, and the paramilitaries on both sides
have laid down (most of) their arms.

Locating Deliberation in the Public Sphere

A more radical discursive democratic response would ask why democracy and deliberation must be joined to head-counting and sovereign authority. Consociationalists take a step in this direction on the head-counting dimension, because they suppress voting's connection to collective decision. But they do not escape the difficulties associated with construction of sovereign authority by constitutional settlement. Consociationalism is therefore vulnerable to Horowitz's pessimism concerning any kind of institutional design in divided societies:

> so many forces favor the pursuit and exacerbation of conflict ... that anything less than a coherent package is unlikely to provide sufficient counterweight to these forces, and yet only partial measures that are doomed to fall short of the coherent package stand a real chance of adoption most of the time. (2000: 262)

Though Horowitz himself recognizes no limits to the reach of this conclusion, his pessimism actually refers only to construction of the formal institutions of the sovereign state. Contemplation of the informal communicative realm might soften his conclusion. Democratic deliberation in a public sphere at some distance from (but not completely unconnected with) the sovereign state can make a major contribution here.

The desirability of locating deliberation in the engagement of discourses in the public sphere in divided societies can draw upon Mackie's (2002) observation that people are rarely seen to change their minds in deliberative forums, and this is especially true in the highly charged circumstances of divided societies. Even if persuaded, it is hard for an individual to admit it, for then credibility is lost. Most conceptions of deliberative democracy require reflection and the possibility that minds can be changed *in the forum itself*. This is unlikely if one's position is tied to one's identity. Locating deliberation in the engagement of discourses in the public sphere avoids this problem because reflection is a diffuse process, taking effect *over time*. With time, degree of activation of concern on particular issues can change. Individuals can shift from partisanship to moderation to apathy, and vice versa, and may even come to adopt different attitudes. Nothing as dramatic as the kind of conversion Mouffe seeks is required. This situation is less fraught than that in decision-making forums where reflection can only take effect in the choices of individuals under the gaze of both opponents and those with a shared identity. As Mackie (2002) points out, deliberation-induced reflection can eventually lead an individual to change his or her mind. But he or she can most easily admit that in a different setting, at another time and place, with different participants, where face and credibility associated with having staked out a position are no longer decisive. Allowing contentious issues to be revisited provides a way for those who have changed their minds to both save face (by not admitting it for the present) and contribute to conflict resolution (by accepting a changed position later).

In relatively well-behaved political systems, the network form of organization can help establish dispersed control over the content and relative weight of discourses, facilitating negotiation across difference. Schlosberg (1999) analyses environmental justice networks in the United States in these terms. These networks arose from a series of local actions and have no centralized leadership. They involve individuals from very different race and class backgrounds, in some cases from groups otherwise quite hostile to each other. Together they successfully changed the content of public discourse on environmental affairs, most importantly by establishing the very idea of environmental justice as a public concern. In societies more deeply divided, the development of networks across divisions could be a greater challenge, given that such societies are divided into blocs with dense within-bloc communication but little across-bloc communication. On the other hand, even in the United States these networks developed across groups which otherwise lived in quite separate worlds, given the informal apartheid of American cities.

Bad Civil Society, and its Remedies

The state should not be conceptualized as the source only of problems for divided societies, and the public sphere only as a benign source of solutions. Public spheres can themselves be segmented, the source of interethnic conflict, and prone to Sunstein's (2002) "law of group polarization" if individuals communicate only with like-minded others. Polarization can be exacerbated by segmented media such as right-wing talk radio in the United States and, most notoriously, Hutu hate radio prior to the 1994 genocide in Rwanda. (The latter was controlled by Hutu extremists associated with the government, so not entirely a public sphere phenomenon.) The fact that sectarian demagogues can flourish therein is exactly why consociationalists seek to silence the public sphere.

Snyder and Ballentine (1996) believe that such communicative extremism is a particular problem in societies emerging from authoritarianism, especially if they lack any tradition of professional journalism. They caution against a liberal free for all in political communication, recommending both state regulation of speech (as in Malaysia since 1969) and NGO intervention to restrict hate speech and promote professional journalism in integrative media.

The problem of what Chambers and Kopstein (2001) call "bad civil society" is not confined to post-authoritarian societies. Focusing on racist hate groups in the United States, Chambers and Kopstein advocate greater income security and social justice, which would mean fewer insecure individuals to be tempted by sectarian extremism. Chambers and Kopstein also guardedly endorse intervention to shape group life through (for example) subsidies to relatively benign organizations that provide services (ibid.: 855). They approve of the role played by Ford, the Eurasia Foundation, and Soros in promoting benign group life in the post-communist world, while recognizing that such efforts may hinder home-grown groups.

Calling the state to the rescue of bad civil society is problematic if the state itself is the instrument of one group in a divided society, or if it is engaged in a homogenization project in order to bolster its own support. A consociational state is not much better if it seeks to suppress engagement in the public sphere. But only a power-sharing state (or a majoritarian government with incentives to appeal to minorities) is in a position to contribute to deliberation across division in the public sphere. The state need not be the exclusive source of solutions here; NGOs and Foundations can play similar parts. And there might even be a role for political theorists when it comes to exposing the false necessities pushed by sectarian groups.

Locating the Public Sphere Transnationally

Engagement across division can be further promoted by transnational aspects of deliberation in the public sphere. Channels of political influence can be extended to and from intergovernmental bodies such as the European Union, international non-governmental organizations, transnational corporations, and other states. Some groups in divided societies have already succeeded in making such links. For example, in response to governmental repression and environmental destruction associated with oil production, the Ogoni people in Nigeria sought help from NGOs based mainly in developed countries. These NGOs in turn pressured their own governments and corporations such as Shell which operate in Nigeria. In Mexico, the Zapatistas in Chiapas have developed an internet-based network of sympathizers. This sort of outreach comes with an implicit obligation to behave according to emerging transnational norms of civility. Snyder and Ballentine (1996: 38–9) recommend transnational intervention to curb the contribution of partisan journalism to hostility in divided societies. Appropriate measures might include professional journalism education, press codes, sponsorship of nonpartisan media, and subsidies conditional on accurate and balanced coverage. They point to the success in Cambodia of a UN media program.

Of course, more negative forms of transnational linkage are possible too, especially by nationalists reaching out to a diaspora. The Irish Republican Army long depended on financial support from Irish-Americans, and much of the Serb diaspora was in the 1990s vocal in supporting nationalism and excusing ethnic cleansing. The opening of channels to a neighboring state of shared ethnicity by a minority is also dangerous, and has historically provided a justification for invasion: of the Sudetenland by Nazi Germany, of Cyprus by Turkey, of Croatia by Serbia. So only outreach beyond shared national identity has a civilizing force. This caveat aside, strengthening of transnational sources of political authority would be conducive to the weakening of the connection between engagement in the public sphere and the deadly contest for sovereign authority.

Any associated weakening of the sovereign state might be especially attractive to those on the receiving end of oppression in countries like Sudan and Rwanda, for whom a centralized state has always brought misery because it has only ever been experienced as the instrument of one segment. Such weakening is also consistent with the increasing conditionality of sovereignty in the international system. NATO intervention in Kosovo in 1999 helped reinforce the idea that sovereignty is not a barrier behind which a state can terrorize sections of its people.

Public Sphere Influence on Government: Loose Connections

Emphasizing the public sphere and its transnational connections as the focus for discursive engagement does not have to mean banning public sphere influence over governmental and intergovernmental decisions. This influence is central to Habermas's (1996) model of deliberative democracy. Habermas endorses diffuse "subjectless communication" in the public sphere, producing public opinion whose influence can then be turned into communicative power through elections, then into administrative power through legislation. This sequence is insufficient for divided societies for two reasons.

The first is that "subjectless communication" is too amorphous when the identity of subjects themselves is the key issue and public opinion is deeply plural. Better under such circumstances to think of engagement across discourses. The second is that elections are highly problematic mechanisms. In any society, competitive elections are largely strategic and symbolically manipulated exercises. In divided societies, the results they register when it comes to the weight of competing groups and of their extremists and moderates depend crucially on the design of the electoral system. And as discussed earlier, a deadly numbers game can result once all sides recognize the possibility of electoral system manipulation. Elections are not the only source of democratic legitimacy, which can also be secured through responsiveness of collective decisions to the relative weight of discourses in the public sphere, which does not have to involve the direct counting of heads (Dryzek, 2001).[6]

Electoral or otherwise, the link from public sphere to collective decision-making ought not to be too tight, because then the deadly contest for sovereign authority resumes. But if influence is absent entirely, there is a danger the public sphere may decay into inconsequentiality. Such decay would undermine the legitimacy of government itself. Between these two extremes one can think of government and the public sphere as being loosely connected, or semi-detached. Discursive engagement in the public sphere can influence collective decisions in many informal ways. These include changing the terms of discourse in ways that eventually come to pervade the understandings of governmental actors. As Habermas (1996: 486) puts it in a moment of expansiveness beyond his stress on elections, "communicative power is exercised in the manner of a siege. It influences the premises of judgment and decision-making in the political system without intending to conquer the system itself." Much of the success of environmentalism and feminism in the late twentieth century can be interpreted in these terms. These two movements provided a new vocabulary – including, for example, the term "environment" itself, which did not exist prior to the 1960s. Individuals versed in these discourses eventually occupied influential positions in government.

Social movements have at times achieved more formal integration into policy-making, though sometimes this has proven a bad bargain if the movement has received mostly symbolic rewards. Genuine as opposed to symbolic inclusion is facilitated to the degree a moment can establish a link between its defining interest and a core function in the state's system of priorities. For example, the alignment of environmentalism with the core economic priority has recently been facilitated in Northern Europe by the idea of ecological modernization, which puts economic and ecological values in a mutually reinforcing relationship, as "pollution prevention pays" (Dryzek et al., 2003). In these terms, a group that defines one side in a divided society has the capacity once included to connect to the core interest of the state in securing internal order. Or at least the group's leadership does, as is clear from the historical success of consociational settlements in Europe. But as this example makes clear, inclusion of group leadership begs some larger questions about adversary versus consensual politics in the institutions of government, and how this affects social learning across difference in the public sphere. Other unresolved questions include the character of the leaders included (radicals or moderates) and incentives for different sorts of behavior once included.

Movement impact from the public sphere via changes in the terms of discourse can occur before, during, and after any such inclusion. In divided societies it is easy to identify rapid change in the terms of discourse that create divisions rather than heal them. For example, Hutu and Tutsi identities hardly existed in Rwanda before Belgian colonial rule. But more benign shifts are possible, as indicated by the rethinking of identity on all sides but especially on the part of formerly dominant whites in South Africa in the 1990s.

Changes in the terms of discourse can be brought about by the power of rhetoric, which can also reach from the public sphere into the state. Such was the achievement of Dr Martin Luther King, Jr in the 1960s. Because King appealed to the emotional commitment of white Americans to symbols such as the Declaration of Independence and the Constitution, he could not easily be dismissed, and eventually the rhetoric forced redefinition of the ways in which dominant liberal discourse was understood. When Nelson Mandela emerged from prison he could have espoused a rhetoric of victimhood and revenge; instead, he developed a rhetoric of reconciliation that looked forward rather than back, with telling effect on the state structure. Arguments honed in the public sphere may be noticed and heeded by state actors, and rhetoricians such as King and Mandela did of course accompany rhetoric with argument.

Positive Examples

Elements of the sort of discursive democratic engagement in a semi-detached public sphere that I am endorsing here can be discerned in some systems. Consider Canada, which features occasional attempts to rewrite the constitution to accommodate the competing aspirations of Francophones and Anglophones, as well as episodes where Quebec looks as though it might secede and then draws back. Attempts to rewrite the constitution normally end in deadlock, frustration, and failure – even if elites manage to bargain a resolution, as in the Meech Lake accords of 1987, which failed to attain ratification due to opposition from Anglophones and indigenous peoples. Failure is generally followed by a period of inaction at the constitutional level. In these periods of inaction, Canada is at its best, because then individuals on the various sides can get back to engaging one another in the public sphere where struggle over sovereignty is not at stake. Political leadership can return to the modus vivendi which makes Canada such a generally successful society. The peace is disturbed only by political philosophers who believe a constitutional solution is required. This is exactly what is *not* required – as should be clear from the lessons of what happens when it is tried.

A second positive example can be found in South Africa's transition in the mid-1990s. Though claimed by Lijphart for consociationalism, that designation applies mainly in terms of the grand coalition that oversaw transition. There was no suppression of engagement across racial and ethnic lines as required by consociationalism's "segmental autonomy." Engagement and reflection were promoted by Archbishop Desmond Tutu's 1995–8 Truth and Reconciliation Commission – which operated at arm's length from the coercive authority of the sovereign state (and withstood legal challenges from both former apartheid President F. W. de Clerk and the African National Congress). The Commission was a deliberative institution whose terms of reference were themselves the product of broad public debate (though the Commission was established under the new constitution). It could offer amnesty and recommend reparations, though the implementation of its recommendations in public policy were haphazard, so its influence on the state may have fallen short of the optimum in the terms I have developed. Perpetrators and victims of apartheid-era political crimes told their stories, and there were some very public episodes of reconciliation between perpetrators and survivors. South Africa also featured mixed-race discussion groups, and efforts to rethink identity in the media, educational institutions, and elsewhere in the public sphere.

Deep division in South Africa did not end with the departure of apartheid. In 1996 a liberal constitution was adopted that specified equal rights for men and women, clashing with the institution of customary marriage in some African communities. Deveaux (2003: 795–800) discusses a series of consultations initiated by the South Africa Law Commission to resolve this conflict, which threatened the authority of traditional leaders. These consultations produced a compromise acceptable to both women's groups and traditional leaders that was reflected in legislation. This compromise entailed some reform to traditional practices while retaining the non-liberal bridewealth payment practice, and avoided confronting the authority of traditional leaders. Deveaux herself does not address the issue, but this avoidance of challenge to the "sovereignty" of traditional leaders may have facilitated deliberative resolution. So although there was a (rare) tight connection between deliberative forum and legislative outcome, this was possible because the "sovereignty" issue was not confronted.

Three Kinds of Failure

To further strengthen the case for emphasizing the engagement of discourses in a semi-detached public sphere in divided societies, consider three kinds of failure in these terms.

The first consists of too tight a connection between public sphere and sovereign authority. The tighter this connection, the greater is the likelihood of a deadly contest over the content of sovereignty. Northern Ireland since the 1990s illustrates this difficulty. Northern Ireland is a highly politicized society, so there is plenty of public debate in the media, clubs, bars, community groups, and so forth. However, the organizations active in this debate have close links to the political leadership negotiating with British and Irish governments over how government in Northern Ireland shall be organized. Community groups, paramilitaries, and politicians are tightly connected. There is great difficulty in maintaining a public sphere at any distance from the sovereignty contest. Heroic attempts have been made by activists to develop networks concerned with issues such as health care, employment, and welfare across the communal divide, but such networks remain precarious in the face of sectarian public spheres joined to each other mainly in the sovereignty contest. Perhaps the most successful anti-sectarian institutions in Northern Ireland today are District Policing Partnerships with representatives from both communities. These boards deal with some of the most divisive and contentious issues in day-to-day life in Northern Ireland, but stay away from the sovereignty question. As such they are elements of a semi-detached public sphere.

A second, very different, kind of failing exists when a public sphere confronts a completely unresponsive government.

Indeed, this kind of polity comes close to failing to be a deliberative *democracy* by definition (unless collective outcomes sensitive to public opinion can be produced in non-state or trans-state locations). Northern Ireland at the commencement of the Troubles in the late 1960s may illustrate this condition. At the time the province had been governed for decades by the Ulster Unionist Party, whose leadership was upper/middle class. The Troubles began as a civil rights movement on the Catholic side. But unresponsiveness and repression on the part of the state played into the hands of the Irish Republican Army, and the social movement gave way to paramilitary action and terror. The struggle stopped being about civil rights, and started being about sovereignty. On the Unionist side, working-class activists denied access by the traditional unionist elite themselves organized in paramilitary fashion.

In divided societies, government that is completely obtuse in the face of movement activism may play into the hands of warlords who prefer violence to the traditional social movement repertoire, exacerbating a sectarian politics that is both irresponsible and violent. Of course, Northern Ireland was already a sectarian state – though beginning in the early 1970s, direct rule from London began to ameliorate this aspect. But even a consociational state that is completely unresponsive to events in the public sphere may be vulnerable. Many factors conspired to drive Lebanon's consociational system into civil war in the 1970s, but one was the complete lack of responsiveness of a system dominated by traditional elites to emerging social forces, particularly on the Muslim side. Warlords could then harness these forces.

A third kind of failure exists when there is no autonomous public sphere worth speaking of. In the case of Austria, decades of a non-contentious party politics and consensus government eventually provided fertile ground for the rise of right-wing populism in the form of Jörg Haider's Freedom Party in the late 1990s. In a very different setting, Yugoslavia under Tito suppressed any kind of contestatory politics, be it within the state or the public sphere, partly for fear of ethnic nationalist mobilization. While the story of the breakdown of Yugoslavia is complex, there were no substantial political forces to stand in the way of powerful figures from the old regime reinventing themselves as murderous ethnic nationalists.

Conclusion

Whether across states, within states, or in the absence of effective states, the divisive politics of identity is largely the result of mobilization through particular discourses. But what is created through discourses can be ameliorated by engagement across discourses. I have tried to show that divisive identity conflicts can be resolved in a discursive democracy that emphasizes engagement in the public sphere only loosely connected to formal government. Contributions to its development could come from:

- deliberative institutions at a distance from sovereign authority;
- deliberative forums in the public sphere that focus on particular needs rather than general values;
- issue-specific networks;
- power-sharing government that does not reach too far into the public sphere
- the conditionality of sovereignty;
- the transnationalization of political influence.

In the early post-Cold War era, violent conflict seemed to be confined to localized zones of turmoil in the world system, affecting core states only at the margins. Matters changed dramatically in 2001. The post-2001 world features a more complex interplay of conflictual discourses on matters of terror and security that reaches far beyond any simple confrontation between "radical Islam" and "the West." In the next chapter I address this complex conflict, and explore a democratic response.

4

Discourses of Error
in the War on Terror

The attacks on the World Trade Center and Pentagon on September 11, 2001 unleashed both military and discursive forces. The military response involved invasion of Afghanistan in pursuit of al-Qaeda and overthrow of its Taliban hosts. The 2003 war on Iraq was justified by the government of the United States in part as pre-emptive action against the forces of terror. (When Iraq's weapons of mass destruction proved to have been already dismantled and its links with terrorist organizations non-existent, the justification expanded to encompass tyranny overthrow and democracy promotion.) Those prosecuting these wars were initially informed by a view of the world populated by formal organizations such as states, military organizations, and intelligence hierarchies, where action is properly instrumental and strategic, and a tangible enemy can in principle be defeated through the conquest of territory and destruction of its physical assets. However, the expanded "war on terror" also involved some discourse-related forces that proved much harder to grasp and control. At the most simple level, a clash of civilizations between radical Islam and the West seemed to be pushed to center stage. Closer inspection reveals a more complex landscape of discourses, with neoconservatism, anarchy, counter-terror, human rights, and market liberalism all important. Resistance to dominant discourses in the global anti-war movement is also significant.

This chapter will examine what happens when a governmental apparatus attempts to navigate such a world. This attempt is fraught with difficulty, and in practice has often inadvertently bolstered the standing of an adversary. Actions on the part of the United States government that seem to make sense in terms of formal organizations and their interactions find their rationality dissolving. Nor is there any easy way to recover this rationality. Those who propose a "war of ideas" to accompany military action recognize transnational discursive forces in the crudest possible terms. Advocates of a more subtle "soft power" approach that recognizes the need to induce others to share one's point of view are more persuasive, but in the end the concept of soft power suffers too many paradoxes to be sustainable. The intent of this chapter is to criticize these mistakes, and to begin to think about how we might do better – and more democratically.

Those who oppose Islamic radicalism, in the US government and elsewhere, have often not quite grasped the importance of the discourse aspect of their enemy. In particular they have failed to recognize the degree to which discourse coordination can in this adversary substitute for more formal and tangible aspects of organization. What happens, then, when actors try to achieve security while neglecting the informal discourse aspects of order and conflict? Confronted with threats, the military and intelligence hierarchies of states target in the first place what they perceive to be other formal organizations, be they hierarchies or networks. Some of these actually exist, as in the hierarchical structure of the Iraqi state under Saddam Hussein. Some of them do not exist in such tangible terms, but are nonetheless imagined in this form – with all kinds of unanticipated and unwanted consequences in the informal discursive realm.

You Can't Kill a Discourse With Bullets and Bombs

The US government's initial response to 9/11 was to find a tangible enemy and conquer it. The main device at the disposal of the US government was its military. It is often said that the military is typically well prepared to fight the last war. More generally, the military is prepared to fight *a* war; and a war needs somebody to point a gun at. A tangible enemy in the form of Afghanistan's Taliban regime held up its hand, and was duly beaten. Its al-Qaeda allies proved more elusive, and the results started to become more ambiguous.

Life would be so much more tractable if al-Qaeda were a hierarchical organization, with Osama bin Laden as the villain from a James Bond script, exercising tight and detailed control over his subordinates. This imagery of tight hierarchy in the enemy continued to exist in Washington. Let me illustrate with just one episode. On March 1, 2003 Khalid Sheikh Mohammed was captured in Pakistan and turned over to the United States. A "senior American official" was quoted as saying that he was al-Qaeda's "chief military operations officer ... at the center of everything" (*Canberra Times*, March 4, 2003, p. 1). Porter Goss, former CIA officer, Republican congressman, chair of the House Intelligence Committee, and later Director of the CIA, said of this event: "this was like the liberation of Paris in World War II" – that is, a key milestone in victory in the war on terror, with a key part of enemy "territory" captured, and the enemy proportionately diminished as a consequence.

This kind of attitude is in the first place simply bad sociology: treating as a hierarchy what is in truth a network (Offe, 2001).[1] A network consists of loosely coordinated cells acting with a great deal of independence from one another. This form is attractive to terrorists in part because the relative isolation of cells makes it harder for outsiders to infiltrate, and insiders to betray. The network extends into and across other radical Islamist groups around the world, such as Jemaah Islamiah in Indonesia. Indeed, destroying the hierarchical aspect of al-Qaeda – for example, taking out Khalid Sheikh Mohammed, if indeed his status is as lofty and central as claimed – may make it an even looser network than it already was. (Though it was already a very loose network.)

What happens if military action is successful to the point

71

where it disrupts the network – that is, the flow of persons, money, materials, and information from one node to another? Does success here indicate that victory in the war on terrorism is closer? Not necessarily. A network may be a physically elusive but not completely unreachable enemy. Slaughter (2004) suggests a transnationally networked response to networked terror, joining "financial regulators, prosecutors, criminal investigators, immigration officials, transport officials and customs agents." Such a networked response would fit uneasily with the George W. Bush administration's more hierarchical desire to dominate interaction with the rest of the world rather than work with it. But even such a networked response would fall short. For a discourse is something else entirely: something that cannot be taken out with bombs, bullets, seizure of funds, arrests, and prosecutions. Al-Qaeda has long had these discourse aspects, which motivated individual radical Islamists to seek out the network, which consequently never had any need to recruit (Burke, 2003: 6). Al-Qaeda was originally named by the FBI in 1998 (in part because US law required a tangible organization that could be prosecuted for racketeering). Burke (2004: 1) suggests bin Laden and his associates "never created a coherent terrorist network in the way commonly conceived." Military success in tangible physical terms may actually strengthen the discourse that remains. The discourse is no longer simply al-Qaeda, because it can encompass those who have never been to Afghanistan, never had any direct communication with Osama bin Laden or his associates;[2] "they merely follow the precepts, models and methods" (Burke, 2004: 1). This discourse may even emerge strengthened, because it now has to do work that was once done by nodes in a network, though any such strengthening for this reason would have to come from the conscious if now dispersed efforts of supporters of the discourse.

A more profound reason why the radical Islamist discourse may emerge strengthened lies in the very actions and rhetoric of those who try to destroy it. Such attempted destruction on the part of its adversaries is a discursive practice very much part of this discourse's own script. For massive military retaliation against the Islamic world is what bin Laden hoped for, to reveal the West in all its oppressiveness, the treachery of governments of Islamic states in all their obsequiousness. These events were seen by bin Laden to be necessary in order to strengthen the discourse, ultimately to move the vast majority of Muslims to rise up against the West and their own corrupt rulers. Of course, this is not what happened. But the discourse can still be a major nuisance well short of such apocalyptic scenarios. To replace the hierarchy that never really was and the network that is under attack, all the radical Islamist discourse needs to do is constitute the actions of a few thousand adherents, not the hundreds of millions that bin Laden hoped for.

Has *this* kind of capacity been diminished by seeming military successes in the war on terror? The answer is unclear. The capacity in question might have been damaged through fear and demoralization, but it might equally well have been strengthened by the mechanisms just discussed.

Bombs and bullets do, then, have unanticipated and often unwanted effects in the discourse dimension of international affairs. Global security issues are home to a constellation of discourses, some that order the world, some that disrupt it. Intelligent action in this situation just has to be sensitive to the content of these discourses, how they take effect, and how they interact with one another. The limitations of a purely military response have eventually been recognized by the government of the United States, which has sought to affect the content and relative weight of transnational discourses (though no policy-makers would put it like this). However, this intervention has been very heavy-handed and counter-productive, for reasons I will now lay out.

A "War of Ideas": Not Good Enough

The global discourse contest has itself been approached by the United States government in a heavily military idiom, with the "war of ideas" a common metaphor. Such a "war" can be approached instrumentally through propaganda offices, planting stories in the press, cultivation of sympathetic reporters, publications, and television networks, staging events for television, and so forth.

The *National Security Strategy of the United States of America*, published by the White House in September 2002, declared that "We will also wage a war of ideas against international terrorism" (p. 6). In July 2004, Lee Hamilton, Deputy Chair of the National Commission on Terrorist Attacks Upon the United States, called for a "battle of ideas" in impoverished countries, to promote "an agenda of opportunity" (*New York Times*, July 22, 2004). At the same time anti-terrorism chief Richard Clarke argued that Islamic radicalism would have to be "defeated in a battle of ideas" (*New York Times*, July 25, 2004). Or as former US Secretary of State Colin Powell put it, "we're selling a product. That product we are selling is democracy" (quoted in van Ham, 2002: 250). Part of the idea is to "rebrand Osama bin Laden as a mass murderer to millions of Muslims" – as *Time* magazine put it, in referring to the administration's employment of a leading figure from the world of advertising (quoted in ibid.: 249). The clash of discourses is therefore treated like the competition of products in a marketplace, to which corporate public relations can be applied. So military metaphors are joined by market metaphors.

Neoconservatives can make use of this kind of approach in their quest to create a new kind of international order in which troublesome states are eliminated. Neoconservatives would rely mainly on military actions such as the invasion of Iraq in the first instance. But they hope that the new order created by force does not have to be maintained by force; indeed, that is the main point of the exercise of force to begin with. Thus they presumably hope that the new order would be stabilized by the development of supportive liberal democratic discourse in countries that have been invaded (though again they would not use the "discourse" terminology). For such development would dramatically lower the maintenance costs to the United States of this new order.

Neoconservatives would presumably see the content of ideas to be disseminated as a straightforward matter, given that they believe that the values the United States is pushing are in fact universal values: liberty, democracy, and free markets.

James Thomson, president of the Rand Corporation, has bemoaned the fact that in the more contemporary "war of ideas" the Bush administration effectively reached the people of the United States, but failed dismally to convince the rest of the world (*Guardian Weekly*, December 5–11, 2002, p. 14). However, this failure is not contingent, a result merely of poor communications strategy. Rather, it follows directly from the communicative aspect of globalization, which means audiences cannot be segmented and given different information and rhetoric. When the President addresses the US media or Congress, he is heard immediately throughout the world. Messages that work so well in one location, and are instrumental to (say) re-election, may have quite different effects in other locations. So when President George W. Bush denounced the evil he saw abroad in the world and the perfidy of erstwhile allies, and announced American resolve against evil, the messages played well at home. Public support for his presidency increased in the face of perceived threat. But at the same time the rhetoric raised the stakes in the global struggle. In making the monetary cost to the United States of responding to terrorist threats so huge, his administration inadvertently helped vindicate the strategy of terror. It is in the interests of many US actors inside government to play up the threat of Islamic terror – thus making its discursive presence more consequential. A cynic might discern more than a faint echo of George Orwell's *1984* here: a government that highlights enemies in order to secure its hold over its own people (see also Archibugi, 2004: 440). What is different is that in our globalizing world, this communicative strategy has discursive consequences beyond the borders – consequences that are usually the exact opposite of those ostensibly sought. The oppositional discourse in the "war on terror" may no longer have any central coordination, if it ever did. The closest thing it does have to a coordinating center is, paradoxically, in Washington, DC. In a unipolar world, the one pole helps coordinate even its opposition – by discursive means.

A centralized monopole is uniquely attractive as a target for terrorists because the consequences of its destabilization are so profound. In contrast, a decentralized political and economic system is much more resilient, because no single target has very high symbolic value or operational significance (Frey and Luechinger, 2004). In 1812 the British burned the White House and America hardly noticed. In 2001 al-Qaeda destroyed the World Trade Center and America and the world were convulsed. The centralization of power in the executive branch of the US government and the imposition of US power on the rest of the world in the wake of 9/11 is everything a terrorist could wish for, making the bull's-eye still bigger.

Worse still, the US government by its actions can create alliances among its opponents. The most egregious example came in George W. Bush's 2002 State of the Union address, which joined Saddam's Iraq, Iran, and North Korea in an "axis of evil." This conjunction was remarkable in light of the long and devastating war fought in the 1980s between Saddam's Iraq and Iran. The speech opened the door to cooperation between Sunni and Shi'ite extremists, who in the past might have been fighting and even massacring one another.

With the endorsement of its brand name by the White House and its allies, al-Qaeda became a uniquely attractive label for all kinds of disparate anti-American individuals and groups around the world. The label is additionally attractive given the powers and capabilities that those who declared a "war on terror" ascribed to their elusive and insidious enemies. Gambetta (2004: 11) refers to a "brand-wagon effect," which in essence means the US strategy becomes to "unite and rule" (the opposite of divide and rule). This rhetorical strategy may have been instrumental to the re-election of George W. Bush, but it is completely counterproductive to US national security. Frey (1988) points out that intelligent governments could combat terrorism by refusing to associate a terrorist act with any particular perpetrator, thus denying the recognition that terrorists crave. US policy toward al-Qaeda is the exact opposite.

"Soft Power": Not Much Better

At the discourse level, US actions and communications after 9/11 served to alienate erstwhile friends and solidify the opposition of enemies, thus producing the opposite of the safety and security that is ostensibly the main concern of US policy-making. A further paradox here is that US actions may well be driven not by mere self-interest, but by a genuine belief that American ideals of liberty, the rule of law, constitutionalism, and the market economy truly are the best model for everyone in the world. The opening sentence of the 2002 *National Security Strategy of the United States of America*, proclaiming a "single, sustainable model for national success: freedom, democracy, and free enterprise," really does represent a deep current in American political thinking, shared by elites and masses, not just by neoconservatives. Many Americans find it difficult to fathom why these ideals are received so differently elsewhere in the world, and why so many foreigners do not see US policy in terms of promoting liberation.

US-based opponents of the unilateralism with which the George W. Bush administration often engaged the world also share these ideals, but consider that they could best be advanced through a more cooperative and solicitous approach. The key concept here is "soft power," the ability to induce others to share one's values and goals, to attract them to one's viewpoint, and to persuade them to engage in supportive actions. The concept is associated in particular with Joseph Nye (2002, 2004), former Assistant Secretary of Defense and Dean of the Kennedy School of Government at Harvard University. Successful deployment of soft power would lead to what Anatol Lieven (2004a) calls "hegemony by consent."[3] Reus-Smit (2004: 65) suggests that neoconservatives can also make use of the idea of soft power, interpreted as a way to spread their conceptions of democracy, freedom, and capitalism. Moreover, the combination of war of ideas and soft power could be interpreted in bad cop/good cop terms, as complementary aspects of a strategy to achieve discourse hegemony – however odd this might seem to proponents of the two doctrines. However, Nye himself is a more solicitous multilateralist, not a neoconservative.

Soft power operates at the levels of both cultural dissemination and public policy. Nye himself stresses the importance of the cultural aspect when he discusses the impact of Hollywood films, other products of popular culture, and the content of global media and the internet (2002: 41–3). He also emphasizes the role of the US higher education system (which hosts students from many countries and disseminates academic products around the globe, including the writings of Joseph Nye). Nye disdains propaganda on the grounds that it lacks credibility. On the other hand, he supports "government broadcasting to other countries that is evenhanded, open, and informative" (Nye, 2003). What Nye has in mind here sounds remarkably like the British Broadcasting Corporation. There is unfortunately no US equivalent to the BBC, whose "evenhanded, open, and informative" aspects have infuriated British prime ministers from Margaret Thatcher to Tony Blair. The difference between "propaganda" (bad) and "public diplomacy" (good) seems in Nye's eyes to boil down to the fact that one is produced by the Pentagon and disbelieved, the other is sponsored by the US Information Agency and so has credibility in the world at large. (Nye (2002: 143) bemoans the assimilation of the US Information Agency into the State Department because it undermines this credibility.)

The other way to pursue soft power through public policy is through sensitivity toward the interests of other actors in the international system (except of course clear enemies). As Nye (2003) puts it: "to the extent that America defines its national interests in ways congruent with others, and consults with them in the formulation of policies, it will improve the ratio of admiration to resentment." "We will have to learn how to share as well as to lead" (Nye, 2002: 41).

Intelligent pursuit of soft power would avoid unnecessary alienation of actual and potential friends. The beginning of the war on Iraq was accompanied by a wave of anti-French sentiment in Washington, DC, as politicians outbid each other to pour scorn on French opposition to the war (including gestures such as renaming "French fries" as "freedom fries" on menus in Congress). Respect for honest disagreement with allies who in the end share most of the values proclaimed as the impetus for US foreign and security policy, but disagree about some of the means, would be more productive in light of soft power considerations.

Maximizing soft power also means leading by example in being an exemplary global citizen, contributing to the supply of global public goods for the economy, security, and environment (Nye, 2002: 143–6). The United States should not proclaim itself above the rules and norms to which others are expected to comply. It may be expedient to declare individuals "enemy combatants" and place them beyond the reach of both US and international law in Guantanamo Bay; but that is a signal that the United States does not in practice respect the human rights supposedly at the core of the "American creed." Similarly, the United States urges the benefits of free trade and unrestricted movement of capital on other countries – this is the essence of the Washington Consensus, by which international economic institutions generally abide. But the US itself often engages in severe protectionism when it comes to politically powerful economic sectors. So US agriculture is heavily subsidized by government, which is bad news for agricultural producers in the developing world, who cannot compete. Serious exercise of soft power would require abandoning these practices.

Unfortunately there are severe limits to the degree the United States can exercise soft power. To begin, many of the agents required to exercise soft power – in particular, producers of popular culture and academics – are outside the control of the United States government. Hollywood is in the business of making money, not disseminating positive images of the United States and its values. Sometimes positive images may be disseminated; sometimes they may not. There are plenty of films that show the dark side of life in the United States. Nye (2002: 11) recognizes that "in the Vietnam era ... American government policy and popular culture worked at cross purposes," but this clash is more pervasive. Academics for their part are a notoriously fractious lot, and among them are critics as well as supporters of various aspects of American values. On the whole they probably support abstract ideals of liberty, democracy, and markets. But the way these are interpreted or applied in particular conferences, journals, lectures, and books varies tremendously, and can be highly critical of the way particular politicians and presidential administrations interpret these same values. For example, postcolonial studies have been influential in US-based research and teaching on non-Western societies. In 2003 this interdiscipline came under attack from conservative members of Congress, who charged it with inculcating anti-American attitudes in students studying other countries. The consequent unwillingness of these students to work for the government allegedly weakened the intelligence and foreign capacity of the United States. In October 2003 Congress passed a resolution to put federal funding for languages and area studies under Title VI of the Higher Education Act under the control of an advisory board that would scrutinize curriculum content for anti-American bias.

A more profound reason why coordinated pursuit of soft power by the United States is so difficult stems from the relative size of the political stakes at home and abroad for US political actors. The stakes at home can be very high, which means that the consequences abroad are either ignored or treated as secondary. Consider the example of agricultural subsidies. These subsidies are dear to the hearts of members of Congress representing agricultural states, not to mention large agribusiness corporations. Who exactly could slash these subsidies? Certainly not Congress, and certainly not presidents aware of the electoral importance of agrarian states. In public debates over agricultural subsidies, the interests of the rest of the world barely even register. Even opponents of subsidies are likely to stress fiscal responsibility and market values at home, not the interests of Third World farmers and basic international justice.

The President's orientation to the rest of the world is often a byproduct of domestic politics. As Henry Kissinger (2001: 15) put it, "what is presented by foreign critics as America's quest for domination is frequently a response to domestic pressure groups." Uncritical support of the Israeli government in its confrontation with the Palestinians makes electoral sense due to the number of Jewish and fundamentalist Christian voters for whom this is a key issue. But this kind of uncritical support precludes any soft power the United States might exercise in the Arab world. As I have already pointed out, messages that play well at home may play very differently abroad. George W. Bush declared he was a "war president," and to the degree he could keep the threat of violent conflict at the front of public attention then his re-election chances were improved. But to many in the rest of the world, a "war president" invocation sounds like a declaration of belligerence. In his second Inauguration Address in 2005, Bush emphasized his continued project for bringing freedom to the world; but with Iraq in mind, the reaction outside the United States was uniformly negative.

Harking back to President Theodore Roosevelt's maxim that the United States should speak softly and carry a big stick, Nye (2002: 157) suggests that "now we have the stick, we need to pay more attention to the first part of his admonition." The problem is, there is no "we" to do this collectively. Instead, there are many American "I"s, be they presidents, members of Congress, lobbyists, corporations, popular culture producers, or academics, whose particular interests point in quite different directions.

A still more fundamental problem with the idea of "soft power" is that it works best to the degree the rest of the world is *tabula rasa* in discourse terms. This is paradoxical in light of Nye's own acceptance of the need to respect non-American points of view, and of the interdependence accompanying globalization (2002: 77–110). The soft power imagery involves dissemination of US values, norms, and viewpoints. But those on the receiving end have their own values, norms, and viewpoints too. The "war of ideas" metaphor at least recognizes that there are other points of view that need to be taken on, though only in terms of opponents that need to be defeated. "Soft power" looks like it recognizes other points of view, and indeed has to take them seriously in order to work. Nye himself points to the soft power that other states, NGOs, and even terrorists such as Osama bin Laden might exercise (2002: 70). However, there are limits to how seriously other points of view can be taken before the whole idea of soft power dissolves.

The important distinction here is between imposition of one's own discourse on the rest of the world, and serious engagement with the discourses of others. Even if accompanied by subtlety and solicitude, soft power will betray the intentions of its proponents to the degree it involves attempted imposition or manipulation. But if it eschews imposition entirely, then it is hardly "power" at all; rather, it is dialogue.

To illustrate the difference between soft power and dialogue, consider the global politics of environment and development. Since the Brundtland Report to the Secretary-General of the United Nations in 1987, *Our Common Future*, the dominant global discourse on these issues has been that of sustainable development. Quite what sustainable development means is a matter of continued contention, though at its heart is the idea that environmental conservation and economic development can be mutually reinforcing. To pull this off will require plenty of coordinated control at all levels of governance, from local to transnational. But the discourse of sustainable development has never made much headway in the United States. As Bryner (2000) summarizes, the dominant response in the United States is "sorry, not our problem" – inasmuch as the sustainable development discourse is even recognized. The politics of environment and development within the United States is still cast in the zero-sum tradeoff, environment versus economy terms established around 1970

(Andrews, 1997). This approach is taken into the international realm too, where the US has, since the early 1980s, been promoting a market liberalism of free trade and movement of capital. Market liberalism is consistent with core US values of a free market – if in exaggerated form. When market liberalism and sustainable development discourses meet in the international arena, the US government typically pushes the claims of market liberalism. At the World Summit on Sustainable Development in Johannesburg in 2002, US representatives and their allies tried to ensure that all references to trade issues came in the form of establishing the priority of World Trade Organization rules over anything that might be agreed at the summit. What we see here may have been soft power exercised with partial success: trade ministers from many other countries lined up to support the United States. But what did not occur was serious engagement between the market liberalism pushed by the United States and the sustainable development discourse so pervasive in the rest of the world, because representatives of the US government never showed any inclination to take sustainable development seriously. So the US tactics produced plenty of resentment and hostility on the part of those who did take sustainable development more seriously, and a proposal that sustainable development measures should be consistent with WTO rules was eventually voted down.

When it comes to issues of security in a world of terror, discourse within the United States is quite different from that in most other countries (except perhaps Israel and one or two East European states). The run-up to the 2003 invasion of Iraq was not accompanied by much in the way of attempted exercise of soft power by the government of the United States. But let us imagine it had been. The events of 9/11 left the United States with a sense of unique and righteous victimhood, which became allied to a renewed and almost messianic nationalism (Lieven, 2004b). Should soft power have been exercised in order to persuade European leaders and societies to accept this discourse? As Lieven (2004a: 31) points out, Europeans in particular remember the catastrophic consequences of their own messianic nationalisms in the twentieth century, and as a result built international institutions like the EU to control them. The reasons for the European position deserve respect; but respect here would involve bringing European discourse into critical engagement with the dominant US discourse. And again, the outcome of any such engagement would have to be indeterminate. There would be no guarantee that soft power would mean the US discourse prevailed. (Lieven himself does not draw the lesson from his own work that I do, ending as a proponent of US exercise of soft power himself.)

The problem with this idea of engagement across discourses is that the outcome is not predetermined. It may be that the values pushed by the United States would emerge on top; but they might not. It would have to be accepted that the public goods of international security, free trade, and international institutions that Nye believes legitimate the US exercise of soft power can be defined very differently by others. This difference would have to be negotiated (Reus-Smit, 2004: 65). This indeterminacy may be a very democratic principle at the international level, just as it is at the domestic level for all those who believe that it is central to democracy that good arguments should be reflected in public policy. But this principle is likely to make even proponents of soft power in the United States uncomfortable. For soft power is still in the end about power, and the right to wield it over others seems backed in the end by the fact that the United States dominates when it comes to the hard power of economic and military resources. To put the matter starkly: one can believe in soft power wielded by the United States, or one can believe in transnational democratic principles. One cannot believe in both.

The Test of Reflexivity

The problematic character of "war of ideas" and "soft power" can be highlighted further in light of the idea that intelligent action must be reflexive. Reflexivity is by definition sensitivity to the degree to which actions themselves help create the contexts for action – that is, they are constitutive of the actor's social situation (Tribe, 1973). To the extent that this situation is defined by the relative weight of competing (or complementary) discourses, action should be sensitive to how it reinforces, undermines, or reconstructs a particular discursive field. Reflexivity requires sensitivity to the extent to which key entities and actors, their interests and goals, the shared norms that constrain them, the relationships that either suppress or empower them, are themselves continually constituted and reconstituted (Berejikian and Dryzek, 2000). Such reshaping is not however unconstrained, because, as pointed out earlier, individuals are themselves situated within a discursive field that constrains who they are and what they can do.[4] Reflexivity is not the same as autonomy, which refers to the capacity of actors to create freely their social conditions. Autonomy connotes the enabling aspect of social structures; reflexivity never forgets that structures and discourses are constraining as well as enabling, and cannot be transcended.

For all their differences, war of ideas and soft power approaches to the navigation of international discourses fail the test of reflexivity. Both are kinds of instrumental action that imply an actor – the US government – can stand aloof from the field of discourses, and manipulate their content and interplay. They both treat power as standing outside discourses, rather than constructed within discourses. They are not alive to the possibility that any dominance of the United States in terms of military and economic power may not translate straightforwardly into the realm of discourses. Soft power advocates treat the world as *tabula rasa* in discourse terms; the war of ideas at least recognizes the discourse of adversaries.

The shared lack of reflexivity of these two approaches means that policies informed by them can have major unanticipated and unwanted effects. Particularly insidious unintended effects can be found in anti-terrorist doctrine.

The 2002 *National Security Strategy of the United States of America* announced a new approach of pre-emption and pre-vention, alongside its declaration of a war of ideas. The United States subsequently followed this doctrine in Iraq and else-where but – crucially – so did other states that picked up on the new discourse. So long as they could brand their adver-saries as "terrorists," the actions of these states could increasingly escape constraints imposed by international human rights discourse, and draw sustenance from the new counter-terror discourse. Israel, Russia in Chechnya, the Philippines, and India in Kashmir could all rebrand their rebels in this way, and receive a kind of international license to oppress dissident populations. In addition, to the degree they could recast their local problems as part of the global war on terror, they could expect to receive support from the Anglo-American powers. However unintended, these consequences endangered the very values that were the ostensible justifica-tion for pre-emption and prevention to begin with – as the September 2002 *Strategy* put the matter in its opening sen-tence, the "single sustainable model for national success: freedom, democracy, and free enterprise."

Democratic Response to an Insecure World

The war of ideas and soft power approaches fail the test of reflexivity because they demand an actor that can stand outside and above the global interplay of discourses. If we look at this interplay from the bottom up, we can locate a more discursively democratic engagement of discourses by a variety of actors in international public spheres that, whatever its other virtues or deficiencies, can more readily pass the test of reflexivity.

We can begin by noting that the capacity to engage dis-courses in critical fashion rather than passively accept them has undergone an increase along with the general movement from discourse hegemony to discourse contestation that I described in chapter 1. In an unreflective world – one where traditions are treated as immutable and taken for granted – the norm is one of obedience to and so reinforcement of dominant discourses. But the ratio of questioning to obedience is not necessarily constant, and would appear to have undergone secular increase in recent decades, certainly in more developed countries, possibly beyond. To corroborate this point, think back to all sorts of impositions upon society that were accepted and unquestioned in Western societies in the 1950s which today would be matters of sharp controversy. These include the massive deployment of nuclear weapons and associated risk of nuclear holocaust, the development and expansion of nuclear power, the construction of freeways without any possibility for public challenge, large-scale urban redevelopment and population transfer with no opportunity for comment by those subject to it, and the adoption of new technologies with no recognition that they might have negative consequences. To the extent that a questioning attitude to such matters is now more widespread, then effective discursive reconstruction can be influenced by agents who will be subject to the discourses in question.

Among the hazards in today's insecure world, terrorism figures prominently. The chances of any individual being the victim of a terrorist attack are statistically quite small. For example, according to the US State Department's annual report, in 2002 there were no terrorist incidents in the United States, 9 in Western Europe, and only 199 worldwide, the lowest total since 1969 (US Department of State, 2003). Yet the risk loomed large psychologically. What is the source of this felt hazard? At one level the answer is obvious: terrorists. But the objective risk from this source is magnified by political leaders and the media, which in turn raises the stakes for states whose legitimacy rests in part on their promise of safety and security, but whose actions in practice are perceived by their own publics and those in other states to undermine safety and security. It is the public perceptions that are crucial here when it comes to legitimacy. Opinion polls show that most people in most countries felt *less* safe as a result of the military successes in Afghanistan and Iraq.

A Gallup International Survey in April/May 2003, immediately after the Iraq war, found that majorities in 42 of 45 countries surveyed believed the world was a more dangerous place as a result of these military actions.[5] Aside from Albania and US-administered Kosovo, the only country that departed from this assessment was the United States (where 48 percent felt the world safer, 36 percent more dangerous). The numbers in countries such as the UK and Australia, whose governments joined the war in Iraq, were little different from countries such as France and Germany, whose governments opposed the war. The more interesting cases are those states whose governments supported the war. It is in these cases that the legitimacy of the state was undermined, as its own population lost faith in its ability to provide safety and security, and indeed thought it might be doing exactly the opposite. Even in the United States, a majority (47 percent to 44 percent) disagreed with the statement that "the threat of terrorism has been significantly reduced by the war." (In the UK 71 percent disagreed with this statement; in Australia 69 percent.[6]) There is also a sense in which *both* sides in the "war on terror" joined in a hazard-imposition complex upon global society, especially given that anti-Western extremism came to be itself sustained in part, however unintentionally, by the rhetoric emanating from Washington and its allies in the media. Further, the *degree* of that threat is in part a social construction by these same agents.

If there has indeed been a secular increase in the proportion of individuals unwilling to resign themselves to the hazards imposed upon them by their own governments – and, perhaps more importantly, the hazards imposed upon them by the governments of other states, such as the US, UK, and Australia – then one would expect substantial public resistance to this hazard-imposition complex. This is indeed what we find, revealed not just as a matter of breadth in opinion polls showing majorities prior to the war opposed to military action, but also as a matter of depth as revealed by protest actions. On the weekend of February 15, 2003 more than ten million people joined in coordinated protests against the impending war in Iraq in cities across the world. In London, for example, the size of the crowd was estimated at around a million – easily the largest protest in British history. Those on the street were only some of those around the world whose uneasiness about and opposition to the war were manifested not necessarily in visible action, but in everyday talk with friends, families, neighbors, and correspondents. They were joined by politicians (including heads of government and of state) from many countries, journalists, political commentators, public figures, and public intellectuals. Stretching a point, the *New York Times* on February 16, 2003 described the protestors as a "new superpower" checking the United States.

International political theorists have been talking for some time about the idea of "international public spheres" – that is, political activists engaged in communicative political interaction across national boundaries, oriented to global public affairs but not seeking a formal share of power in states or in international government (Cochran, 2002). More than ever before, in February 2003 a transnational public sphere was tangible and visible on the world stage, its influence extending into the governments of several countries.

A cynic might say here that in the end the protests and broader global discontent amounted to nothing: after all, they did not stop the war. But this would be to focus on the instrumental effects of these protests and miss the constitutive ones. While the protestors failed in instrumental terms, they may have been more effective in reflexive terms: that is, in the way they help reshape the global constellation of discourses. Moreover, the protests in Western countries (along with positions taken by governments such as France and Germany) helped to show the Islamic world that the peoples of the West were not against them, even if a few Western governments appeared to be. In the face of that reality, it became harder for Islamic extremists to maintain the rhetoric of a titanic clash between the West and Islam. It also became harder to argue that terror should be directed against the ordinary people of the West, most of whom were so clearly not in favor of war against Iraq, let alone against the Islamic world more generally. This did not of course prevent attacks against the ordinary people of the West (for example, in Madrid on March 11, 2004 and London on July 7, 2005). However, even al-Qaeda eventually showed responsiveness to Western public opinion. In a tape broadcast in April 2004, Osama bin Laden referred to "public polls" in European countries showing opposition to the Iraq war, and so offered a "truce" with European countries if they were to leave Iraq. With that statement al-Qaeda began to look like a more conventional sort of terrorist organization with which Western governments have long dealt – one that makes negotiable demands.

It is very difficult to demonstrate the impact in the Islamic world of the anti-war public sphere in the rest of the world – but no more difficult than it is to demonstrate the impact of forced regime change in Afghanistan and Iraq on the global strength of Islamic extremism. However, this comparison is not quite appropriate. For transnational discursive democracy located in the public sphere is not directed against any particular enemy. Rather, it ought to be evaluated in terms of how it can influence and reconstruct processes of global governance, and so help combat the global insecurity to which many sides contribute. In the wake of the Iraq war begun in 2003, it is obviously not decisive when it comes to global security issues – but neither can it be ignored by conventional powers such as states. Try as it might, even the world's sole remaining superpower ignores the global public sphere opposed to it at its peril. This public sphere is a formidable discursive entity whose role is not appreciated by those in Washington promoting either war of ideas or soft power. To the extent the United States seeks to ride roughshod over the kind of global public opinion this public sphere generates, the maintenance costs of a world order to the liking of the US will be very high indeed. When in unilateral mode, the US government finds it relatively straightforward (though not costless) to bypass or override formal international institutions such as the United Nations and its agencies. The international public sphere is more elusive, and not so easily vanquished.

The kind of diffuse engagement of transnational discourses

I have described can, then, much more readily pass the test of reflexivity failed by "war of ideas" and "soft power" alike. The reason is that participants in international public spheres cannot plausibly be tempted by the idea that they can control and manipulate the world of discourses from the outside. The constellation of discourses that constitutes the world can be remade from the bottom up through intentional political action (and not just from the top down through unintended consequences of the sort that created a discourse of counter-terror that justified the behavior of repressive governments). Participants in this process should be under no illusions about the constraints under which they operate. To get anywhere at all, they have to take seriously and engage the discourses that they encounter, rather than treating them as enemies to be vanquished in some war of ideas.

Democrats, Tyrants, and Terrorists

This endorsement of discursive politics in an insecure world might seem to beg the question of how to engage actors who are outside the boundaries of civil discourse and who cannot conceivably be brought within it. Discursive democracy can flourish to the degree the world is ordered by contending discourses amenable to reflective engagement. The world that we currently inhabit is not always like this. The standard liberal approach to such questions is to say that those who do not respect the basic rules of the game such as tolerance should not be surprised to find that they are repressed at tolerant hands (see, for example, Popper, 1966, vol. I: 265). As the nineteenth-century liberal John Stuart Mill put it in his *On Liberty*, "despotism is a legitimate mode of government in dealing with barbarians, provided the end be their improvement." Translating this liberal argument to the international level means that aggressive states and other actors that defy international norms of acceptable behavior to their own population and to other countries should not be surprised to find that military action is taken against them.

Indeed, these are the terms in which the United Nations was established after World War II.

Comprehensive theories of liberal democracy within states and of the international system usually specify some sort of punishment mechanism to keep transgressors in line. Within the liberal democratic state, it is a system of law, which liberal multilateralists want to replicate at the international level, and empower transnational law-enforcement authorities (ranging from UN troops to the International Criminal Court). For realist theorists, it is a matter of powerful states meting out punishment as they see fit in light of their strategic interests and their stake in system stability using whatever means are most expedient – be they economic sanctions or military action. Neoconservatives would be happy to endorse such punitive actions, though they care much more than do realists about the effects on the internal political structures of states on the receiving end. (Realists are concerned only with threats to system stability, not with political or humanitarian issues inside states.)

Transnational discursive democracy does not mean averting one's eyes from actors in the international system purveying violence and death, and holding to a naive faith in the possibilities for dialogue in every situation. Much of the analysis in chapters 1, 2, and 3 was concerned with the roots of violence and misery in contending discourses; and the degree to which such violent contention might yield to more productive engagement across boundaries. Still, it remains the case that there may be actors beyond the reach of such engagement. As I write, the main example would be North Korea, seemingly immune to any sort of international communication. Thus any problems North Korea generates for the international system – for example through its possession of nuclear weapons – are not easily processed through discursive means. Yet the very extremity of the North Korean example also indicates its oddity: in an increasingly interdependent world, agents of disruption that set themselves up in splendid sovereign isolation are increasingly rare (and the price of isolation is impoverishment). Most agents of disruption, be they the masters of the military-industrial complex or Third World dictators, on closer inspection reveal at least some sensitivity to collective opinion and the sanctions it can motivate, however much they would like to evade such constraint.

Agents of disruption that cannot secure splendid isolation operate within a context provided by the global constellation of discourses, whether they like it or not. This applies even to transnational terror operations. I have argued that these operations are now coordinated in large part by the discourse they share. And if this is so, then part of the response to them must operate at this discourse level. This is recognized, if in very simplistic form, by the "war of ideas" strategy – which is unfortunately likely to have exactly the opposite of its intended effect, by raising the standing of its target. As I have argued in this chapter, it is also possible to think about confronting (say) Islamic radicalism through discursive means that operate in more democratic fashion. This does not mean unconditionally welcoming terrorists into dialogue, or being nice to those who plant bombs on underground trains or fly airliners into tall buildings. Though even here it should be noted that former terrorists sometimes go on to successful political careers, be it as partner in peace negotiations with an adversary (Michael Collins), Prime Minister of Israel (Menachem Begin), membership in power-sharing government in Northern Ireland (Gerry Adams), or Nobel Peace Prize-winner (Yasser Arafat). It remains possible to think about how the global constellation of discourses might be reconfigured in ways that diminish the supply of volunteers for terrorist actions.

Highlighting discursive democracy is not the same as advocating an international system free of formal institutions in which only the interplay of discourses produces outcomes. Discursive democracy can coexist with a variety of governance mechanisms, including those that involve punitive action against war criminals and terrorists. Indeed, there is no need to think of transnational discursive democracy as a model of democracy. Rather, transnational discursive democracy is a process of democratization that can work in the context of any formal organizations and institutions and other governance mechanisms that happen to exist, be they states and their militaries or international organizations. (See Dryzek, 1996: 4–6, on why it is generally better to think in terms of processes of democratization rather than models of democracy.) I have of course highlighted the importance of contending discourses in both explaining the way the international system works and proposing a particular approach to its democratization. This does not mean that only contending discourses matter when it comes to the production of international outcomes, and that intelligent action in the international system should be solely a matter of rearranging the interaction of discourses for the better. But in an insecure world, seeking to rearrange the discursive field surrounding justifications for violence in ways that minimize the supply of those willing to commit such acts is crucial. The only issue is how democratically this is done; and I have argued in this chapter that undemocratic ways of doing it are likely to have exactly the opposite of their intended effect.

Conclusion

Recognition of the importance of the pervasive contestation of discourses in international affairs has major consequences for how we think about issues of security and conflict in a world where the threat of terrorism looms large. The traditional national security apparatus and military hierarchy of states find it hard to handle these aspects of the world. Recognition of the importance of contending discourses occurs in crude form with proposals for a "war of ideas" to accompany military action, but such a "war" will probably not impress friends, while helping to galvanize enemies. The idea of "soft power" is superficially more promising, but on closer inspection it is very difficult for the United States in particular to exercise soft power in consistent and coordinated fashion. But even if it could act in the manner required, there is a paradox at the heart of the soft power concept. To the extent it is "soft," it has to take seriously the concerns of other actors in the international system. But to the extent it is "power," it cannot take these concerns seriously enough to consider changing the discourse it is engaged in propagating. Thus there is a conflict between the pursuit of soft power and minimal principles of democratic debate. In a democratic world, this conflict can only be resolved to the degree that soft power is set aside in favor of more egalitarian engagement across discourses of the sort central to transnational discursive democracy.

5

Contesting Globalization

Market liberal globalization is the major contemporary discourse that can stake a claim to international hegemony, in that it sets the terms of reference and range of possibilities in international affairs. While globalization can mean many things, the dominant aspect is economic, corporate, or what Wolf (2004) calls "liberal," at least when it comes to international political economy. Globalization in this sense reaches into many other areas of life (environment, social policy, human rights, even international security). It is especially powerful when allied with market liberalism and a Promethean approach to environment, energy, and resources. Francis Fukuyama's (1989, 1992) "end of history," with the world dominated by a single global model of liberal democracy plus capitalism, could look very much like this (though it wouldn't have to, because the end of history could also accommodate more social democratic national systems). Market liberal globalization's claim to hegemony would threaten much of what has appeared in previous chapters about democratic negotiation of the engagement of competing discourses, at least when it comes to issue areas that relate to economics (and most of them do). So in this chapter I will look at the possibilities for contestation of globalization itself. This in turn will open the door to thinking about the democratization of globalization.

96

Globalization as a process involves the integration of economic, social, cultural, and political transactions into a single system, rendering old boundaries increasingly irrelevant. International capitalism is at the forefront. According to Held and McGrew (2000: 3), the key elements of globalization include "action at a distance; time–space compression; accelerating interdependence; a shrinking world; ... global integration, consciousness of the global condition." Increased interchange when it comes to trade, investment, finance, communications, media, ideas, education, and people all make contributions. Recognition of globalization processes does not necessarily mean that we actually have an integrated global socio-economic system, or are even close to it. Globalization should be taken to mean the set of forces that, if taken to its conclusion, would produce such an integrated system; and the discourse of inevitability that accompanies such forces.

Even skeptics such as Hirst and Thompson (1996), who point out that the world economy is only partially and very unevenly integrated, recognize the power of globalization as ideology, or discourse.[1] Beck (1999) distinguishes between the process of globalization and the ideology of globalism. In developed countries, the discourse takes effect through policymakers accepting the "no alternative" policy logic it promotes, and adopting market liberal policies. In less developed countries, it sometimes takes the heavier hand of the World Bank or International Monetary Fund imposing privatization, deregulation, free trade, and budgetary austerity conditions in return for financial assistance. These conditions are sometimes called the "Washington Consensus," because they represent the received view of the United States Treasury, the IMF, and the World Bank, all based in Washington, DC.

In this chapter I explore the power of globalization as process and as discourse. Globalization leads to a decline in the formal authority of organizations, and so the capacity of states in particular to control life within their boundaries. What is less often noticed is that this decline can also apply to non-territorial organizations such as corporations and even international governmental organizations (IGOs). The reach of market liberal globalization discourse is long. But there are countervailing developments that could enable a more discursively democratic negotiation of globalization.

Globalization and the Decline of Formal Authority

The seeming hegemony of globalization is secured in part by its capacity to undermine differences between states that would otherwise be busy either securing their own strategic interests or pursuing different political models. Globalization means that the intensity of the interactions across the boundaries of organizations increases. They face a "runaway world" in Giddens's (2000) terms, a context that threatens to elude both understanding and control (though Giddens himself celebrates the positive aspects of globalization). As Beck (1999: 11) puts it: "Globalization denotes the processes through which sovereign national states are criss-crossed and undermined by transnational actors."

In this familiar kind of presentation, the organizations being undermined are states, whose territorial boundaries are eroded by increasing flows of trade, investment, finance, people, communications, ideas, and culture, which cannot easily be controlled by national governments. Transnational corporations increasingly operate without reference to any particular national base, manufacturing, buying, and selling in many countries. Corporations can threaten to take their operations elsewhere if a country tries to impose labor standards, environmental regulations, or taxation not to their liking. Financial institutions are also transnational, and instant electronic communications mean vast flows of money can cross national boundaries with ease and immediacy. Regional groupings such as the North American Free Trade Agreement (NAFTA) and European Union take on functions once performed by sovereign states. Countries joining global economic organizations such as the WTO, IMF, and World Bank agree to abide by the rules of such organizations and accept their decisions. Even the United States, which often exempts itself from the economic recipes it urges upon others, in 2003 removed a tariff introduced in 2002 to protect its steel industry. The WTO ruled against the tariff and a threat of EU retaliation would have targeted products made in states that were marginal in presidential election terms.

Globalization is not just economic. The internet facilitates communication of ideas and information across national boundaries, and authoritarian governments find it hard to censor the information reaching their populations (though some still try). National governments are called to account by international human rights standards and find it difficult to hide their abuses from the global media. Political activists organize transnationally in non-governmental organizations that can exert coordinated pressure on national governments and transnational corporations. Cultural transnationalization follows international media corporations and the dissemination of brands, images, newspapers, books, films, and television programs. People are also on the move across national boundaries, as migrants, asylum seekers, and refugees, as tourists, or as privileged cosmopolitan citizens of the world (like me).

Globalization does, then, limit sovereignty and the control capacities of states. Moreover, the flows associated with globalization increasingly cut across the boundaries of organizations that are not defined on a territorial basis. We could even reverse Beck's quote to say that "Globalization denotes the processes through which transnational actors are crisscrossed and undermined by sovereign states" – though we would have to add that transnational actors are undermined by other transnational actors and local actors too. For example, a transnational corporation's affairs are not just a matter for its management and its shareholders. They are also subject to the influence of the governments of countries where it operates, particular regulatory agencies, community activists, IGOs, NGOs, the media, management consultants, banks, auditors, other corporations (in the form of interlocks as well as competition), and politically motivated consumers.

A good analysis of the Royal Dutch-Shell Corporation in

these terms is presented by Frynas (2003). In the mid-1990s Shell suffered two major shocks to its image. The first involved the case of the Brent Spar, a redundant oil-storage platform in the North Sea that Shell initially wanted to dump in the deep waters of the North Atlantic. A transnational campaign and boycott led by Greenpeace forced Shell to change its plans. The second concerned Shell's operations in Nigeria, where the company's association with a military dictatorship that imprisoned and executed activists trying to get a better deal from oil production on their land (notably, Ken Siro-Wiwa of the Ogoni people) brought international scorn. Shell undertook a major repositioning exercise in response to these shocks. Shell expanded its renewable energy operations, established a Social Responsibility Committee, sponsored community environmental projects in the UK, began a dialogue with human rights organizations, withdrew from the Global Climate Coalition of corporations opposed to any action to restrict fossil fuel use, and became active in the World Business Council for Sustainable Development.

Interdependence and interconnectedness are key defining features of globalization (Held and McGrew, 2000: 1). What they mean is that hierarchical organization is replaced by network organization, captured in Castells's (1996) image of the "network society." Unlike a hierarchy, a network has no apex or center of control. Rather, it has multiple nodes that interact without any command relationship. A network is an informal arrangement that can encompass a variety of actors: elected leaders, public officials from different governments and units, political activists, representatives from NGOs and interest groups, and from corporations. Membership can be fluid, depending on the specifics of the problem at hand. Solutions are produced by and in the network, often in ways that blur the boundary between public and private sectors. Castells applies this idea to the global economy, where companies are themselves networks and their interactions create further networks: "Networks converge toward a meta-network of capital that integrates capitalist interests at the global level" (1996: 475). International financial networks are crucial: "Money has become almost independent from production ... by escaping into the networks of higher-order electronic interactions barely understood by its managers" (ibid.: 504). Again, what we see here is that globalization overwhelms not just the control capacities of states, but also the control capacities of corporate managers and international financiers. Formal organizational charts and models such as those using game theory that stress the strategic and considered choices of actors as they confront each other are equally useless in capturing networked organization.

These sorts of developments suggest that globalization makes it increasingly hard to distinguish between the "inside" and "outside" of organizations. Of course, organizations such as corporations and national governments continue to exist. But they find it harder to confront one another as unified entities, given how enmeshed they are in interactive social systems.

Globalization Discourse

Market liberal globalization discourse operates through what Hay (1998) calls the "logic of no alternative." On this account, states must reduce or eliminate tariffs on imports, accept the local operations of global corporations on their territory, harmonize their financial systems with international norms, integrate their financial systems with those of other countries, float the exchange rate of their currency (or join transnational currencies like the Euro), gear production to global rather than local markets, facilitate global communications by providing infrastructure (such as airports), harmonize their educational systems so qualifications will be recognized internationally, make international travel easy, control social welfare spending so as not to have tax rates above internationally competitive levels, and regulate trade unions to prevent them making labor too expensive and so uncompetitive. All these policies can remain controversial within states, and all clearly benefit some interests and hurt others. Political leaders who support market liberal policies to begin with can use the rhetoric of "no alternative" or "globalization means we must do it" to justify and enact policies that they would support anyway. For example, in 2005 a report by the Organization for Economic Cooperation and Development (OECD) found that Australia's marginal income tax rates were too high to be competitive. This provided support for those in government who wanted to cut income taxes for domestic and partisan reasons. Some countries, such as the Netherlands and Denmark, have managed to resist aspects of the recipe (for example, by reaching deals with union federations to moderate wage demands in return for retaining a relatively generous welfare state). The discourse of globalization can play out somewhat differently in different sorts of states (Marsh and Smith, 2004), but its pressures exist everywhere.

Market liberalism, the dominant economic recipe accompanying globalization, involves a set of understandings about the desirability of free trade, the unimpeded movement and operation of capital, privatization, the deregulation of markets, and the undesirability of an interventionist state pursuing non-economic goals. This discourse pervades the understandings of policy-makers in most states, who fear the negative consequences of its violation: disinvestment, capital flight, and disapproval of the WTO, World Bank, or IMF (Hay and Rosamond, 2002). Such punishment occurs in large measure because the punishers themselves subscribe to market liberalism, and so act according to the scripts the discourse provides them with. Formal organizations may still exist in this kind of setting, and it may look as though they are making authoritative decisions. The IMF, WTO, and World Bank have consciously adopted the precepts of market liberalism as recognized in the Washington Consensus, and apply those principles in rulings to bind states. So the IMF or World Bank will make deregulation and privatization conditions of "structural adjustment" loans to a country in financial and economic strife; the WTO will adjudicate trade disputes between member states according to some basic principles of free trade.

Punishment of transgressor states here is *not* just or even primarily imposed by centralized police officers. The WTO, for example, has a small staff and can only intervene in a very small number of trade disputes. Punishment is mostly decentralized in the myriad choices of corporations, accountants, investors, and bankers, who are coordinated mainly by the discourse they share. This discourse will, for example, lead them all to shun a country seen as deviating from the economic recipe that market liberalism provides. So it does not matter whether such deviations are "objectively" bad in their impact on economic performance. All that matters is that market actors believe they are bad, which means that deviations cannot be pursued if market confidence in a country or region is to be maintained. For example, in the wake of the 1997 East Asian financial crisis, the government of Indonesia felt it had to follow the policies laid down for it by the IMF, not because it believed those policies were the right ones, but because they were consistent with market liberal doctrine, and so necessary to secure the confidence of investors, banks, and corporations (Dalrymple, 1998). The discourse turns out to play a key role – both in giving organizations like the WTO an enforcement capacity, and in giving substance to the punishments that market actors can exact by coordinating their behavior around market liberal precepts. All this is carried out at minimal cost (except for those at the receiving end of punishments). Shared discourses come much cheaper than organizational commands.

Toward Deliberative Globalization

Deliberative globalization would be the opposite of "the logic of no alternative" and the associated hegemony of market liberalism. It would subject particular aspects of globalization, and the policy prescriptions that seem to accompany them, to critical scrutiny. Market liberal precepts and prescriptions might conceivably find themselves validated, but they would have to do so through engagement with other discourses, not just on their own economistic terms. This scrutiny would not have to be confined to the formal institutions of national governments such as legislatures. Indeed, there are reasons to suppose such formal institutions may not be the ideal place for open deliberation on these sorts of issues, because of their ties to executive decision that feels bound to meet the demands of market liberal globalization (Dryzek, 1996). Deliberation in the broader public sphere is less constrained because less tied to executive decision. And to the extent that public spheres can transcend national boundaries, then this sort of deliberative globalization is itself a kind of globalization process, as it involves integrating communication across national boundaries.

Many kinds of discourses other than market liberalism are intertwined with transnational networks. For example, a network of human rights activists and officials is organized around a particular rights discourse. Those networked on environmental issues often share a sustainable development discourse (though this is contested from a number of sides, by green radicals, Prometheans allied with market liberalism, and those subscribing to a discourse of limits and survival – see chapter 1). In chapter 4, I pointed out that discourses can also substitute for networks in coordinating the behavior of geographically dispersed actors. For example, disruptions to the al-Qaeda network mean that the actions of its adherents are coordinated largely by the discourse they share, rather than instructions, messages, or materials flowing between nodes of the network.

Globalization enhances the possibilities for deliberative negotiation of networked governance and its associated discourses through its facilitation of communication over large distances and across organizational boundaries. Indeed, to some analysts "time–space compression" is the essence of globalization, as individuals in all parts of the globe are brought into closer contact with one another. Cheap telecommunications, the internet, transnational media networks, and inexpensive travel all play roles here. Ease of communication means ease of dissemination of a discourse.

Thus the al-Jazeera television network disseminates a particular discourse on international affairs to the Arab world, a
discourse that is highly suspicious of US and Western
motives in the region, highlighting Arab death and destruction in a way the Western mass media generally shrinks
from. The Murdoch media empire disseminates a right-wing
version of world affairs through its print and television out-
lets in numerous countries. Social movement activists
make extensive use of the internet to disseminate their concerns, as well as staging events – such as protests at meetings
of the IMF, WTO, and World Economic Forum (WEF) – that
the more conventional media pick up and disseminate
(often with very particular slants). The importance of such
flows to discourse dissemination – and discourse contestation
– is confirmed by the (increasingly ineffectual) efforts of
authoritarian regimes such as China to obstruct them.

Within the international system there are of course institutions interested in either shutting down such critical debate
or imposing a more hegemonic and economistic version of
globalization (for example, some large corporations, the
WTO, IMF, and US Treasury). Anti-corporate globalization
protests of the kind that began in Seattle in 1999 have at least
had the effect of opening up a space for deliberation about
globalization – meaning it is no longer a unified set of prescriptions before which all governments and all people must
bend.

Are there ways in which the "governance" aspect of globalization might be democratized? This governance aspect is
stressed by social democratic supporters of globalization such
as Giddens (1998), as opposed to the unimpeded economic
integration of the liberal economic globalizers. However,
there were signs that beginning in the late 1990s, even the
enthusiasts of market liberal economic globalization associated with the IMF and World Bank had recognized the need
to involve NGOs in the implementation of their designs,
rather than riding roughshod over them (Putzel, 2005: 7).
The term "governance" as opposed to "government" highlights
the fact that it proceeds in the absence of sovereign centers of

power of the sort that characterizes states (or at least once did). So it is not organizations under a formal mandate that are doing most of the work in transnational problem-solving (Rosenau, 1992; Young, 1994). As Young (1994: 14) puts it: "governance does not require the creation of material entities or formal organizations of the sort we normally associate with the concept of government." The question of exactly what mechanisms contribute to international governance is left open-ended, at least for Rosenau (1998: 32), for whom "Global governance is the sum of myriad – literally millions – of control mechanisms" with no "grand logics." In practice, discussions of governance in international relations emphasize regimes (institutions and rules that actors abide by),[2] shared behavioral norms (such as the rules of war), cooperative arrangements between states, and reciprocal understandings.[3] Slaughter (1997) suggests that transgovernmental networks (made up of officials from similar departments in different states, with input from corporations and NGOs) can work more straightforwardly and effectively than formal IGOs. Sometimes networks can be seen contributing to global public goods in benign fashion – as, for example, when global insurance companies communicate with environmentalist NGOs and environmental ministries on measures to reduce the risk of extreme weather events resulting from climate change. Networks of organized criminals and terrorists stand at the other end of a continuum, producing mostly global public "bads."

International relations scholars typically care little about democracy in the international system itself, and so rarely distinguish between governance mechanisms with democratic potential, and those without. Transnational governance is, like democracy itself, decentralized. However, decentralization does not necessarily entail democracy: perfect markets are decentralized but not at all democratic. The kinds of networks that Castells (1996) stresses are financial and corporate, steered by money rather than any semblance of popular control, let alone deliberative democracy. And of course organized crime and terrorist networks are hardly known for their deliberative or democratic qualities. Networked governance does not have to mean *democratic* networked governance. Why then might transnational governance be amenable to democratization?

Networked governance is not devoid of democratic opportunities. Hajer (2003: 175) refers to "transnational, polycentric networks of governance in which power is dispersed," escaping the sovereign state. Novel issues such as those pertaining to genetically modified organisms or crises in food safety (such as BSE/Mad Cow Disease that hit Britain in the late 1990s) have no obvious institutional home for their resolution. Sometimes novelty is a matter of novel technology. Advances in human genetic technology generate all kinds of moral issues that both ethicists and governments alike are ill-equipped to handle. Agricultural biotechnology for its part generates new sorts of issues concerning trade-related intellectual property rights (TRIPS) that confront international trade regimes (and the WTO, among others). Responsibilities for action are ill-defined, as is the range of actors with legitimate interests. Hajer speaks of an "institutional void" that exists when there is no formal bureaucratic allocation of responsibility for a problem. Thus problem-solving on such issues is accompanied by negotiation of rules and norms to govern the interactions and responsibilities of activists, advocates, and public officials. Dispersed decision-making, venue-hopping (as advocacy groups target different parts and levels of government in pursuit of their interests), and fluid problem definitions are pervasive. Under such circumstances, multi-centered and multi-level dialogue is much more feasible than sovereign control (see also Hajer and Wagenaar, 2003), and this points toward more deliberative negotiation of globalization.

Cracks in the Globalization Monolith

Democratic possibilities can be glimpsed in globalization. In part, these possibilities arise from the fact that globalization

107

itself is not quite the monolith it first appears; or at least, that cracks are appearing in the monolith. These possibilities are as follows:

1   The very fact that in developed countries globalization discourse appears as a "a logic of no alternative" suggests that the discourse of economic globalization is not in fact hegemonic. The idea of a logic requires that arguments need to be made on behalf of policies consistent with the market liberal aspect of globalization. If the discourse were truly hegemonic, it would be taken for granted by all relevant actors, and there would be no need to argue for policies consistent with it. This situation would be portrayed by followers of Michel Foucault as "neoliberal governmentality," with all relevant subjects in the global system constituted in compliant ways conducive to the demands of the market liberal economic system. These actors would seemingly be free, but in practice always exercise that freedom as consumers and market actors. There have been discourses with hegemonic reach like this in the past – for example, the discourse of industrialism (which I have stressed when discussing environmental affairs).

2   Globalization involves the development of transnational governance networks, which, like democratic decision-making, are decentralized. Of course, decentralization is not a sufficient condition for democratic control; but it is a necessary one. The lack of centralized authority in transnational governance is at least one less impediment to democratization.

3   The more important transnational or global governance becomes, the more its legitimacy will have to rest on some notion of democracy. This is because in today's world, democracy is the *sine qua non* of legitimacy. This demand for democratization has appeared in the context of the European Union, whose "democratic deficit" is now widely recognized as being in need of remedy. The fact that this pressure took so long to emerge in a

very governmental international body is, however, a bit discouraging from the point of view of democracy. For more elusive and intangible governance mechanisms such as networks are less visible and less obviously centers of power that need legitimating in the eyes of publics.

4   Globalization now has its own resistance movement, most visibly in protests that have routinely accompanied global economic summits (especially the WEF, G8, and WTO meetings). While initially scorned by insiders and ridiculed by much of the media, the movement has succeeded in opening up a space for debate about the winners and losers from globalization, and the effect of economic globalization on public goods such as environmental quality – globally, and more locally.

5   The communicative aspect of globalization has made it easier for activists to communicate across boundaries, thus leading to the creation of international public spheres. These spheres are key components of transnational democracy, because they are sites of generation of transnational public opinion that can in turn seek to influence centers of power, be they corporations, national governments, or international government bodies. The fact that such international activism is derided by Wolf (2004) as "antiglobalization. com" points to the role of the internet in facilitating such activism.

6   Globalization has its own internal tensions, especially when it comes to the role of the state. At one level, globalization points to the decline of the autonomous state – whether authority goes from the state to international markets or to international governance mechanisms such as networks. At another level, globalization requires states to implement its precepts. It may require a strong state to be in a position to impose market liberal precepts on its society; but a state being undermined by transnational governance may find it hard to muster the necessary authority. This is most likely to be a problem for states on the periphery of the world economy.

7 Novel problems may initially be characterized by an "institutional void." While much can happen to fill any such void, democratic or otherwise, its very novelty means that traditionally powerful actors have not had time to set up exclusionary arrangements, meaning that a variety of actors has the capacity to advance their own definitions and interpretations on a situation.

None of these seven items represents anything capable of bringing down the citadel of corporate globalization, certainly not on its own. Dominant actors, be they large corporations or the institutional enforcers of market liberalism such as the WTO and IMF, have some very substantial resources at their disposal. However, navigating a globalizing world requires a particular kind of intelligence that, perhaps surprisingly, currently dominant actors may in the end find harder to apply. This sort of intelligence is reflexive in character, sensitive to the constellation of discourses in which it operates. In the next chapter I will address this kind of intelligence in detail, and try to show that its increasing importance could open up substantial opportunities for transnational discursive democratization.

6

Reflexivity and Resistance

Accompanying globalization are not only global markets, but also governance mechanisms, networks, and discourses that transcend national boundaries (see chapter 5). In this chapter I will show that this kind of world requires a particular kind of reflexive intelligence. This requirement applies to all actors, from superpowers to citizens. It turns out that civil society actors such as NGOs can often negotiate these arrangements in reflexive fashion more straightforwardly than can states and (especially) corporations. This possibility in turn highlights ways in which corporate globalization is not necessarily hegemonic, but can actually be countered by some associated opportunities for transnational discursive democratization.

In chapter 4 I introduced the idea of reflexivity as a test failed by "war of ideas" and "soft power" projections in the war against terror and associated endeavors. Both see the world of discourses as capable of manipulation from the outside, by the government of the United States. Both fail to recognize the existence of discourses in the world out there that will produce unintended outcomes from their interaction with the messages disseminated by actors based in the United States following the precepts of these two approaches. Reflexive actors are aware of their status "inside" the world, and of the fact that their actions and messages help constitute or re-constitute the world in which they are operating. Even the most routine action helps perpetuate the discourse in which it is located by affirming the precepts of that discourse (for example, a financial transaction reinforces the monetary system).

In this chapter I will explore further this idea of reflexive action in international affairs. In the first instance, intelligent reflexive action means simply that actors – including traditionally powerful ones, such as states – develop an enhanced breadth of awareness of the consequences of their actions. However, reflexivity cuts deeper to the extent that all actors, down to the level of individual political activists, develop such a critical awareness of their circumstances. Such awareness, the essence of reflexive modernization (Beck et al., 1994), means that traditionally powerful actors, up to and including superpowers, find it increasingly hard to bend the world to their liking, because dominant scripts come to be questioned. One manifestation of reflexive modernization comes in the form of transnational resistance movements – to war and economic globalization in particular. Such movements therefore cannot be dismissed as inconsequential or simply disruptive. They can be consequential in affecting the content and relative weight of global discourses. They can help constitute global public spheres that influence (though never directly control) international outcomes; and as such have a place in a transnational discursive democracy. I will show that there are crucial ways in which reflexive action is actually a more straightforward matter for civil society actors (such as NGOs and political activists) than it is for states and corporations. If this is the case, then a focus on reflexivity can actually shift the balance of power away from states and corporations and toward civil society. While civil society is not necessarily a paragon of democratic virtue (and can be home to some very bad things, as was seen in chapter 3 on divided societies), this shift entails a redistribution of power within the international system in a direction conducive to transnational democratization.

The Idea of Reflexive Intelligence

If actions constitute situations, then intelligent actors should reason constitutively as well as instrumentally, such that constitutive concerns should often override instrumental ones. Constitutive reasoning is central to reflexive action. Instrumental rationality is the capacity to devise, select, and effect good means to clarified and consistent ends. In reasoning constitutively, an actor does not just ask the instrumental question, "Does action X help achieve goal Y within the context of the world as it is?" Instead, the actor asks, "Does action X help constitute a world I find attractive?" This distinction between instrumental and constitutive reasoning has been made by Laurence Tribe (1973) in the context of US environmental law and policy. Tribe's worry was that the strategies and arguments pursued by environmentalists were effective in achieving immediate goals (cleaner air and water, some wilderness preservation) but that, in so doing, they made the kind of social paradigm shift ultimately desired by most environmentalists less likely. For these arguments involved accepting the basic structure and value system of industrial society as given, and appealing to values of human health and wellbeing in order to justify the policies advocated. The constitutive effect is to provide support for an industrialist paradigm that many environmentalists themselves believe is ultimately untenable.

All actions have both instrumental and constitutive effects. Instrumentally, an environmental organization can tout the benefits of tropical rainforests as a genetic storehouse for pharmaceutical companies in a bid to get those companies to help lobby for forest protection. Constitutively, such action helps reinforce the idea that rainforests have only commodity value to industrial society – thus bolstering the discourse of industrialism. So if, for example, pharmaceutical companies were to discover that genetic engineering means they no longer need the rainforest, it is at the mercy of other productive uses. Short-term effectiveness may have been purchased at the expense of long-term discourse shift away from industrialism. Such a shift is required to protect tropical forests more securely. Actors ought to think long and hard about how their actions affect the relative power of the different discourses present and available.

Actions help undermine or constitute discourses whether actors like it or not. For example, when in the early 2000s the US opposed or claimed exemption from the International Criminal Court, renounced the Geneva Convention in its treatment of "enemy combatants," and withdrew from multilateral treaties such as the Kyoto Protocol on climate change, it reinforced the discourse of anarchy (in the sense of the absence of central authority entailing an ever-present threat of violence and disorder) in the international system, thus making this anarchy more real. The consequence was discursive reinforcement of the international anarchy in which opponents of the US might find refuge – surely the last thing that leaders of the US intended. Such consequences are too important to be ignored – which is exactly what happens when there is a narrow instrumental focus on immediate goal-attainment, to the exclusion of constitutive reasoning.

Now, "realist" theorists and practitioners of international relations believe anarchy is an immutable feature of the international system to which states, the key actors, must resign themselves as they pursue security. If they are right, the issue of constitutive reasoning would never arise. Statecraft for realists (such as Henry Kissinger) is a matter of skilful operation under anarchy. However, if realists are wrong and anarchy is not immutable, the instrumental acts of realist policy-makers may end up undermining the stable international political order that is the fragile accomplishment they prize. Such undermining may be the last thing that state leaders have on their minds, but so long as they behave according to realist precepts, that is exactly what they will do – because they will construct other states as potential enemies, thus making enmity more pronounced. Thus realism is nothing more or less than a self-fulfilling prophecy; the anarchic world that realists accept with weary resignation is in truth a creation of states behaving in accordance with realist precepts, if

114

only as a matter of habit rather than conscious choice (George, 1994: 223). These actors could create different situations, and so ultimately a different world, but do not do so. To create different situations does not require coordinated collective action (of the sort advocated for example by liberal multilateralists); all it requires is that actors think through the consequences of their individual actions (see Berejikian and Dryzek, 2000, for more details). To create a different world is a somewhat larger matter of reflexive behavior on the part of some critical mass of key actors.

Reflexive Action in Practice

Can we find examples of international actors behaving in intelligent constitutive fashion? Alexander Wendt (1992: 419–21) uses the example of Soviet leader Mikhail Gorbachev in the 1980s to show "how states might transform a competitive security system into a cooperative one." Gorbachev signaled that Soviet identity and interests had changed through actions such as withdrawal of forces from Afghanistan. His behavior was consistent with the idea that identities are bound up with discourses that can change, not something primordial and fixed (see chapter 3). Gorbachev wanted to tie Soviet identity to a discourse of cooperation as opposed to Cold War confrontation in international affairs, and in so doing helped constitute a different kind of international system. (Gorbachev did not of course intend the subsequent demise of the Soviet Union, though the causes of that demise remain debatable, and were not a simple consequence of his foreign policy.)

The Gorbachev example illustrates constitutive reasoning and reflexive action on the part of a state. But non-state actors can also act in this fashion – and later I will suggest they may be able to do so more easily than states. Consider the following case that illustrates one state actor behaving reflexively, one economic actor behaving instrumentally, and one civil society actor behaving reflexively.

115

In 1995 the Shell oil corporation was faced with a decision about what to do with the Brent Spar, a redundant oil storage platform in the British sector of the North Sea oilfields. Shell determined that the most environmentally acceptable method of disposal within reasonable cost constraints would involve towing the platform to deeper waters in the North Atlantic and sinking it. The British government agreed. Environmental groups opposed this decision. Greenpeace in particular organized boycotts and demonstrations against Shell service stations in a number of European countries. Greenpeace activists occupied the Brent Spar to obstruct its movement. The British government prepared to use force to dislodge the activists, and urged Shell to stand firm. Much to the chagrin of the British government, Shell gave in to the environmentalist pressure, and agreed to take the Brent Spar to Norway, where the platform would be dismantled and its parts disposed on land. It soon became clear that disposal on land would probably involve greater environmental costs than sinking the Brent Spar in the North Atlantic (for details of this case, see Rose, 1998).

Of the three key actors involved in this incident, one acted instrumentally, and two constitutively. Shell's actions were purely instrumental. First the corporation sought a disposal option that appeared environmentally acceptable while not imposing undue costs on the company. With the damage to its image and sales caused by the Greenpeace campaign changing the financial calculations, Shell reversed its decision to favor a different disposal plan. The British government had no real material stake in the issue, but wanted above all to see a discourse of state sovereignty and respect for private property (such as oil platforms) respected and reinforced. This consideration explains British government anger at the seeming usurpation of its prerogatives by Shell and Greenpeace, together acting in "paragovernmental" fashion.

Instrumentally, Greenpeace for its part should probably have accepted disposal in the deep Atlantic, as among the various options this promised the least environmental damage. Critics of Greenpeace were quick to describe its actions as expedient and unscrupulous, for the incident provided the sort of publicity on which Greenpeace fundraising thrives; and Greenpeace did later suffer adverse publicity for getting key facts wrong. Constitutive considerations pointed Greenpeace in a different direction. Greenpeace sought to advance an environmental discourse under which redundant industrial installations cannot be dumped in the nearest available hole, but have to be dismantled and (ideally) recycled. Moreover, any advance made by a discourse like sustainable development which promotes the influence of transnational civil society at the expense of the state is in Greenpeace's interest too (though in the interests of many other actors as well).[1] So a closer look at the constitutive effects of Greenpeace's actions reveals their moral dimension. First and perhaps foremost, the whole notion of sustainability is advanced to the degree a potential dumping ground is declared off-limits. Given Greenpeace's long-standing concern with protecting the integrity of marine environments, disposal of the platform in the deep North Atlantic could be seen as the thin end of a (discursive) wedge legitimating deep-ocean dumping. In addition, the transfer of influence from the state to transnational civil society has an ethical as well as an instrumental aspect, because it is a component of the sustainable development discourse, as well as a building block of transnational democracy (though Greenpeace probably has little concern for any such democracy).

Reflexive Modernization

The degree of critical awareness that reflexivity demands intelligent international actors should acquire might appear to be a tall order. Yet the world may be changing in a direction which makes this kind of awareness increasingly feasible. The idea of reflexive modernization has achieved prominence in the recent work of Ulrich Beck, Anthony Giddens, and Scott Lash (1994; see also Beck, 1992), among others. Reflexive modernization is a process whereby individuals become aware of the traditions, rules, and understandings that govern their lives – and see them as potentially open to change. Individually and collectively, people become more committed to the idea that they can chart and reshape their own future, rather than mostly adjusting to the tide of events. In this light, the industrial society with which we have become familiar over the past century or more is only semi-modern, for it treats large areas of life as off-limits to conscious collective control. Foremost among these, Beck argues, are the trajectories of the market economy, science, and technology. These areas have long been granted a privileged position in policy-making, in that they were treated as having a momentum of their own to which states and other actors could only adjust. Certainly they were immune to popular control.

To Beck, we now stand at the threshold of transition from the semi-modernity of industrial society to modernity proper, or reflexive modernity. The main reason is that ordinary people have become all too conscious of the risks generated by industrial "progress." Moreover, they have come to distrust the technologists who have helped to generate these risks, and the states and corporations that have employed them as risk apologists. The risks Beck has in mind are those associated with nuclear, biotechnological, chemical, and climatological hazards. For Beck, politics is increasingly about the production, allocation, and distribution of these risks – as opposed to the issues of income distribution and class conflict which preoccupied politics in industrial society. At issue here is not just the emergence of a new dimension of political conflict, but rather the displacement of one kind of politics by another. Given that risks fall upon rich and poor alike (though Beck is wrong in thinking they fall *equally* upon rich and poor), cross-class political mobilization becomes much easier than it was under the class-divided politics of industrial society. While the theorists of reflexive modernity have generally emphasized politics at the domestic level, especially as it involves economics, science, and technology, many of the same hazards and responses to them arise at the international level. Many hazards are especially acute at the international level, including risks associated with nuclear weapons, war, terror, and counter-terror.

There is no guarantee that reflexive modernization will produce the kind of democratic politics for which its theorists yearn. Indeed, we have seen that reflexive traditionalization is also a possibility, as a critical reaction to globalization and modernity leads individuals to seek shelter in fundamentalist religion, ethnic identity, or nationalism (see chapter 1). Still, some aspects of contemporary circumstances are propitious – and this is no less true in international society. The Cold War provided a structure to which policy-makers in the superpowers and other states believed they had to adjust. The structure of the Cold War was sometimes softened, but more often hardened, by the (often unwittingly) constitutive actions of states, and it took a degree of heroism (such as that of Gorbachev mentioned earlier) to escape the discursive bonds of the conflict. With the end of the Cold War, there ensued more leeway for constitutive action and reasoning, and it looked as though there was a world to create, as well as to accommodate. Matters changed after 2001 with the polarizing character of the "war on terror" and associated military actions. But while the post-2001 international system seemed dominated by a discourse bunker shared by US unilateralists and Islamic radicals, it also featured transnational resistance to the perceived hazards imposed on the rest of the world by those in this bunker. The international public sphere that arose in opposition to the war on Iraq in 2003 was a popular reaction to the perceived risks that the United States in particular was imposing upon the world. Resistance and reflexivity can be linked – a point I will develop shortly, and address the consequences for the development of transnational democracy.

Constraints on Reflexive Action

Reflexive action is engaged from within a system, not from the outside. That system inevitably imposes constraints on action as well as providing opportunities for action. Indeed, it is the presence of these constraints which makes action "reflexive" as opposed to "autonomous," for "autonomy" implies the absence of constraints. In discourse terms, the structure of what Bourdieu (1993) calls a "discursive field" helps constitute who actors are and what they can do – though this field is also amenable to reconstruction through their actions.

Other analysts are more likely to highlight the hard structural constraints of a situation. We have seen that realists argue that states simply must behave in certain ways – or risk catastrophic consequences as other states take advantage of them. While we have also seen that "anarchy" can take different forms depending on the attitude of state policy-makers, there are potential uncertainties involved in destabilizing a familiar context such as the Cold War by taking a different attitude.

It is also possible to point to some hard structural constraints imposed by life in the international political economy. The economic, social, and environmental policies of states must stay within certain boundaries if they are not to upset the confidence of investors and financial institutions, leading to disinvestment, capital flight, and financial panic. Policies must be tailored with the interests of investors and financiers in mind. As we saw in chapter 5, those constraints exist in large measure because key actors in the global political economy subscribe to a particular kind of economic discourse. But the fact that such constraints are ultimately discourse-inflected does not make them any less materially real from the perspective of the policy-makers of nation-states. Such policy-makers may find it hard to act reflexively, even if they recognize the possibility of such action in principle. The continued ascent of market liberal discourse since the 1980s has intensified these kinds of constraints. Market liberalism as a structural constraint is in many ways more severe than Hobbesian anarchy for, as we have seen, anarchy can be constituted in different ways, and softened if not eliminated by the reflexive actions of states.

Market liberalism resists such reconstitution because its automatic punishment mechanisms (disinvestment and capital flight) stand ever ready to bring potential resistors back into line (Lindblom, 1982). Yet the structural power of market liberalism, massive though it may be, is not total; for market liberalism is indeed a discourse as well as a structural force, and so what market liberalism *means* may be subject to reconstruction at the margins. For example: market liberalism may always mean putting economic principles above environmental ones. But if advocates of environmental values can establish the idea that conservation can actually benefit business profitability – an idea central to the discourse of ecological modernization (Dryzek, 2005: ch. 8) – then policies that promote conservation will not necessarily meet with recoil from the market.

Reflexive Action is Hardest for Corporations, Tough for States, Easier for Civil Society

In light of the constraints I have detailed, the capacity to act reflexively proves to vary in important ways across different kinds of actors in the international system. When it comes to the distribution of power in the system, a skeptic might argue that reflexive action does not necessarily change matters, on the grounds that traditionally powerful actors, up to and including superpowers, can still have substantial and perhaps even dominant constitutive effects in the discursive realm. Some actors are more capable than others when it comes to disseminating meanings and discourses (Weldes and Saco, 1996), and in the past this has led to attempts by dominant states to impose ideological hegemony on the world. These attempts continue today when it comes to the war of ideas and soft power emanating from the United States. However, in today's world, the results of such attempts are just as likely to be unintended and counter-productive as intended and productive. When it comes to the world's current remaining superpower, those effects include reinforcement of the

121

discourse of anarchy (as a result of actions such as the invasion of Iraq in defiance of majority opinion in the United Nations, and without Security Council approval, opposition to the International Criminal Court, and withdrawal from the regime to control global climate change). The world can be remade for the worse, especially if realists and neoconservatives get their way.

Intelligent international actors, and especially intelligent superpowers, can and should do better. Perhaps enhanced awareness of the reflexive aspects of international action could lead dominant actors to consolidate power by acting more intelligently in relation to the global constellation of discourses, so that their constitutive effects become a matter of design rather than accident.

The good news for those interested in a more egalitarian distribution of power in the international system is that traditionally dominant actors actually turn out to be the most constrained when it comes to possibilities for reflexive action. All actors, be they states, international bodies, corporations, activists, ordinary people, or non-governmental organizations, are constrained by the discursive field in which they operate, that helps condition who they are and what they think. But only states and corporations are also subject to the kinds of structural constraints discussed in the previous section. States simply have to pursue security as a priority (unless they are lucky enough to be part of the developed West, and so facing few threats from their neighbors) and must keep markets happy. Corporations simply must pursue profit – often with an eye on the short term.

The Brent Spar example discussed earlier is revealing here. The Shell corporation was not at all interested in constitutive reasoning, changing course to announce the redundant oil platform would be dismantled on land rather than dumped in the deep ocean as soon as bad publicity and a consumer boycott threatened its profits. The British government tried to stay the course when it came to reaffirming discourses of sovereignty and private property, preparing to use force against the Greenpeace protestors occupying the platform. Sovereignty and private property actually help constitute, respectively, security and economic imperatives, especially in the long term. Greenpeace and its activists were subject to no such constraints, and so had much greater freedom to act in reflexive fashion in pursuit of the environmental values the organization cherishes. Instrumentally, Greenpeace gained little (for deep ocean disposal was probably no worse environmentally than dismantling on land). But Greenpeace's actions helped reinforce the idea that deep ocean marine environments should be off-limits to dumping.

This uneven distribution of the capacity to act reflexively, biased it seems in favor of civil society actors who are disadvantaged when it comes to more conventional sources of political power, has important implications for the wellsprings of transnational democracy. If transnational democracy requires decentralized power in the hands of reflexive actors, then civil society actors should be central. Corporations are at the other extreme, limited in their reflexive capacity by the need to pursue profit. States lie somewhere in between, constrained by security and economic imperatives, but also capable of interpreting these imperatives in long-term fashion (as in the case of the British government confronted by the Brent Spar problem), and occasionally being able to find some freedom of maneuver.

I have highlighted the role of civil society actors relatively unconstrained in the capacity to act reflexively. Yet one should treat with great caution any connotations of virtuous civil society activists confronting and eventually transforming established relations of power in the international system. For sometimes civil society is not at all civil. In a divided world, it can also feature groups whose intentions toward one another are hostile, even murderous – as seen in earlier chapters on the "clash of civilizations" and divided societies. But those chapters also showed that deep divisions of this sort can themselves be approached in discursive and democratic fashion.

Resistance is Fertile[2]

Seen through the prism of the capacity of civil society actors for constitutive reasoning and reflexive action, transnational resistance movements take on added significance. Think of anti-corporate globalization movements in recent years. From Seattle in 1999 to Genoa to Melbourne to Evian in 2003 and beyond, economic summits such as meetings of G8, the WTO, and the WEF are now routinely accompanied by carnivals and protests. The protestors themselves are part of a far larger transnational public sphere questioning economic globalization. The protestors and critics were at first widely ridiculed by governmental leaders and the mainstream media alike for being a disparate bunch with no common program, only a range of contradictory concerns. These concerns included the protection of the environment and jobs in the developed world, an end to the exploitation of cheap labor in the Third World, and better terms of trade for the developing world. But the protestors and critics were successful in getting a range of issues onto the agenda of these summits and the international organizations and governments that attend them. As Joseph Stiglitz (2002: 20) puts it: "the protests have made government officials and economists around the world think about alternatives to the Washington Consensus policies as the one true way for growth and development." Indeed, the critics' lack of a coherent program from the outset was actually a sign of the degree to which they were participants in the decentralized construction of a counter-discourse to oppose global market liberalism. So from the point of view of more diffuse and democratic control over the global constellation of discourses, this absence of a program was actually a positive sign. As Young (1997) points out, difference can be a resource when it comes to democratic communication.

Eventually, the protestors were joined by Stiglitz (2002), former Chief Economist at the World Bank, and before that Chair of President Clinton's Council of Economic Advisors. But even as one of their leaders he felt he could not bend the market liberal discourse that held them in its grip. Only when he left those organizations could he join the discursive struggle against market liberalism. As Stiglitz himself recognizes, the ground for this intervention was prepared by all those who had participated in protests against globalization, joined NGOs that questioned market liberalism and its international institutions, wrote critical pieces in newspapers, magazines, or on the internet, or even just participated in critical talk about the global political economy. The cumulative weight of small interventions in the discursive field can be substantial – which is just how it should be, in a democratic world of discursive reconstruction. It may take substantial time and effort for this weight to be felt, but as Max Weber put it long ago, politics is often about the slow boring of hard boards. That is especially true in the international system; think for example of the eight years it took for the Kyoto Protocol on climate change to receive ratification from a significant set of states and come into force – and nobody claims Kyoto is anything more than a tiny beginning in any attempt to confront the climate change issue. So discursive democracy is by no means unique in this respect.

Ironically, resistance can actually contribute to the production of order in the international system. Protests in Western countries against the Iraq War in 2003 helped moderate polarization between the West and the Islamic world. Protests against corporate globalization have led to dominant economic institutions thinking about ways to ameliorate impacts on those losing from privatization, deregulation, and budgetary austerity. This stabilizing impact of resistance is paradoxical in light of the fact that those resisting often seek the destabilization of established distributions of power. Conversely, dominant discourses can be forces of disruption rather than order. Market liberalism is the dominant discourse in the global economy – but it is quite capable of disrupting the political stability of states subject to its ravages. Neoconservatism dominated US security policy in the George W. Bush presidency – and destabilized the Middle East and beyond. In this light, resistance can act as a stabilizing corrective in the system.

125

Reflexivity and Democratization

Reflexive modernization means that ever-increasing numbers of actors are capable of influencing their social relationships rather than simply accepting them. The basic idea of reflexive modernization is that individuals are increasingly unwilling to take for granted the traditions in which they have been socialized, or to accept risks imposed upon them as inevitable accompaniments of progress. This increasingly diffuse potential for consequential action itself is a force for democratization in the world – simply because it increases the number of people capable of exerting influence in international affairs (however far short it might fall of global political equality). Diffuse reflexive action has in common with liberal multilateralism (which I will address in the next chapter) the idea that the creation of a better international system will require action by many actors. The essence of intelligent reflexive action in international politics is attention to the contextual restructuring that seemingly limited decisions can produce. This provides support for the basic liberal multilateralist desire to promote social change in the international system. The world can indeed be remade for the better, just not so straightforwardly as liberals believe.

Diffuse reflexive action has a major advantage over multilateral construction of international institutions. It can help bring into being changed situations without the need for coordinated collective decision-making. Required only is that actors reason through the broader consequences of their individual decisions and acts. More systemic change (that is, change in the discursive field ordering the international system) can then come about as a result of reflexive action by some critical mass of actors. And it is this potential which paves the way for a more democratic approach to international affairs – including the security issues which have so often seemed off-limits to any semblance of democratic control (see the discussion of anti-war protests in chapter 4).

This possibility of diffuse reflexive engagement points directly to a transnational discursive democracy, featuring increasingly widespread capacity to influence the balance of discourses in the international system. Of course, there are many countervailing forces – including those targeting the discursive realm. These countervailing forces include, for example, war of ideas and soft power approaches (see chapter 4), geared to imposition of the ideology of a dominant actor. But as pointed out in chapter 4, transnational discursive democracy can more easily pass the test of reflexivity that war of ideas and soft power approaches fail. For discursive democracy is relatively immune to the kind of hubris that supposes the world of discourses can be transcended and manipulated from the outside. It has to recognize as a matter of its own democratic commitment that interventions come from myriad actors located within the discourses of the world, without the capacity to step outside them. Effective engagement with the world has to be reciprocal and democratic. When discursive democracy and reflexive action are joined, agency (the capacity to act) can be distributed more widely than is possible in war of ideas or soft power approaches, which centralize agency. There are points at which widespread engagement concerning the terms of discourse is possible, as the examples of transnational social movements I have discussed illustrate.

This kind of engagement is not the only available response to either global insecurity or runaway economic globalization. An international project of much longer standing seeks to address such issues by building formal international institutions. That project is liberal multilateralism, which in its recent cosmopolitan version has also acquired a democratic twist. I will address the diminishing prospects for this project in the next chapter.

7

Governing Discourses: The Limits of Liberal Multilateralism

In previous chapters I have emphasized the degree to which the contemporary international system can be captured in terms of contending discourses, and the ways transnational discursive democracy can be pursued in such a world. Obstacles to discursive democratization include discourses and identities that can seemingly only underwrite confrontation (be it across civilizations or within divided societies), unilateralism that seeks (whether through wars of ideas or soft power) only to displace one discourse by another, hegemonic discourses (such as globalization attached to market liberalism), understandings of the international system that ignore its discourse dimension (such as realism), and even networked governance to the degree it evades discursive scrutiny. I have tried to show how all these obstacles can be overcome. A project of long standing that takes issue with some of the same foes is liberal multilateralism. In this chapter I will show that though its heart may often be in the right place, liberal multilateralism can also be quite problematic in a world of competing discourses, and especially so when it comes to thinking about discursive democracy. These criticisms apply largely to the way liberal multilateralism has been practiced since the end of World War II, though they have a large "in principle" component too (that is, they apply to liberal multilateralism in principle). My criticisms apply mainly to the

128

degree multilateralism is accompanied by the introduction of administrative bodies and constitutions. While multilateralism does not have to be like this, it does represent the path of least resistance, and the painstaking way that multilateral institutions are constructed often mean they have to be like this. In the next chapter I will show that some contemporary attempts to democratize multilateralism, especially through cosmopolitan democracy, do not entirely solve the problems I identify.

Multilateralism involves creating international bodies, agreements, and rules through negotiation on the part of states that will be subject to the arrangements in question, who agree to be bound by these arrangements (Ruggie, 1993). In its dominant formal manifestations, multilateralism reaches for an ideal that is heavily constitutionalized; and part of the price of any success is the creation of administrative structures that operate on very traditional hierarchical lines. Both constitutionalization and administrative rationalism turn out to be problematic to the degree the engagement of competing discourses matters.[1] They sit uneasily in a globalizing world of growing complexity, interdependence, and discursive engagement of the sort outlined in chapter 5. These problems are especially troublesome for those who want to project liberal multilateralism into a more thoroughgoing cosmopolitan international order.

The Multilateral Idea

The bipolar confrontation of the Cold War yielded to a unipolar aftermath that provided substantial scope for unilateral action on the part of the United States, even before the terrorist attacks of September 11, 2001 led to increased emphasis on coercive strategies to bend the world to its liking. However, the Cold War was predated by, and coexisted with, a multilateral approach to the construction and operation of global institutions designed to secure peace, prosperity, and cooperation in solving joint problems. This approach persisted in practice into the new century, even if it did so in the very noticeable absence of the United States. (Though even the United States remained a selective multilateralist, for example when it came to the World Trade Organization.)

Liberal multilateralism really got into its stride at the end of World War II. This period saw the creation of the United Nations and its agencies, the Bretton Woods system for international economic coordination overseen by the International Monetary Fund and World Bank, and the General Agreement on Trade and Tariffs (GATT). The United States obviously had the most important say in the design of these institutions, and, given its dominant economic and military position in the aftermath of the war, was able to secure a world order very much to its own liking. However, the US sought the consent of other governments in institutional construction (though many were hardly in a position to refuse as a consequence of their devastation in the war). In stark contrast to its early twenty-first-century behavior, the US agreed to be bound by the rules of the institutions that were established. By the 1990s the US was using its financial leverage to dominate IMF decisions, using the IMF to promote market liberalism against alternative developmental models (such as East Asian cooperative capitalism), thus diluting the multilateral qualities of that particular institution.

Post-World War II multilateral institutions essentially only dealt with two areas: economics (Bretton Woods and the GATT) and collective security (the United Nations), and these remained the cornerstones of multilateralism. But with time, the world became ever more thickly populated with international governmental organizations and the various treaties that set up principles for their operation. Some were regional (like the European Union or Association of Southeast Asian Nations), some global. Some were formal organizations (such as the International Labor Organization and World Trade Organization), others were better described as "regimes." A regime is an institutional arrangement for the promotion of international cooperation, containing "principles, norms, and rules" as well as "decision-making procedures"

(Krasner, 1983: 1). A regime may contain a formal organization – so, for example, the WTO is central to the global trade regime. But regimes as institutions can also feature regularized but not necessarily formalized understandings, rules, and obligations. So the world trade regime also rests on shared understandings about peaceful commerce, the legitimacy of pursuit of private property, the degree to which states can regulate imports and exports, and so forth. The Bretton Woods financial system worked for the global economy from the late 1940s until the early 1970s because of a particular kind of liberal discourse that all parties subject to it shared, and which could enable them to cope with contingencies (Ruggie, 1982). Although regime analysts rarely use the term "discourse," international regimes generally need to rest on a supportive discourse.

In the immediate aftermath of the attacks of September 11, 2001, it looked briefly plausible that liberal multilateralism would flourish and coordinate global responses to terror. Secretary-General George Robertson invoked the Mutual Defense Clause of the NATO founding treaty for the first time, declaring that a NATO member had been attacked, and that it was the task of all member countries to help respond. From France, on September 12, *Le Monde* famously announced in an editorial that "we are all Americans." In a flush of enthusiasm, Ulrich Beck (2001) believed that the United States now realized that its response to terror could only be multilateral. For as the community of those affected by the risks of terror was global, so, he argued, must be the political organization in response, culminating in an international system of criminal justice that all states would have to join.[2] A multilateral response would have involved strengthening global and regional institutions, and crafting actions (including military ones) through them. This response might even have followed the suggestion of Frey and Luechinger (2004) about confronting terrorism by dispersing power; because centralization heightens the symbolic value of targets associated with the dominant power, as well as increasing the disruption that a successful strike can cause.

131

The Limits of Liberal Multilateralism

These multilateralist hopes were soon dashed as the US retreated into unilateralism (Prestowitz, 2003). As Calhoun (2002) puts it, "what could have been an occasion for renewing the drive to establish an international criminal court and the multilateral institutions needed for law enforcement quickly became an occasion for America to demonstrate its power and its allies to fall into line with the 'war against terrorism'." Indeed, "allies" hardly had the status that word connotes, being expected to accept roles as subordinates. In the build-up to the Iraq invasion, the George W. Bush administration essentially told the UN Security Council to go along with its wishes with the promise that if it did not, the US would take whatever action it saw fit anyway. Reus-Smit (2004: 8) calls this "the diplomacy of ultimatum and exit." US opposition to multilateralism extended to renunciation of the Anti-Ballistic Missile Treaty (originally negotiated with the Soviet Union) in order to pursue space-based weapons systems, non-ratification of the Protocol on the Involvement of Children in Armed Conflict, and opposition to international agreements to restrict chemical and biological weapons and land mines. In short, the US opposed any multilateral restraints on its own freedom of action, often irrespective of the benefits such institutions and agreements would yield for others (or indeed itself). While intensifying after 2001, American unilateralism is actually grounded in a long political tradition that cannot accept any authority higher than the Constitution of the United States, which is seen as embodying "foundational American values . . . both immutable and inherently superior to anything the world has to offer" (Hathaway, 2000: 133).

The invasion of Iraq in 2003 was justified by American neoconservatives in democratic terms, in the expectation that liberal democracy could be transplanted into Iraq, which would then become a more peaceful actor on the international stage. On the face of it, this justification could be shared by liberals looking forward to a world in which such actors could enter cooperative institution building. But neoconservatives themselves have no interest in establishing institutions above or across the nation-state, and the military means they prescribe undermine any such project. Held (2003) condemned the war as a "return to the state of nature" (in Hobbesian terms), producing a "crisis of legitimacy" for existing international institutions, which are "cast aside ... if they fail to fall in line with the interests of the most strong." Held's (2003) response to both 9/11 and the Iraq war is to reaffirm the need for "an alternative strategy for a rule-based and justice-oriented, democratic multilateral order." But he allows that this alternative is "temporarily lost from view. We must fight to regain it." Held adheres to a strong version of liberal multilateralism that is also far more democratic and justice-oriented than actually existing multilateral institutions.

Multilateralism did however persist in the face of setbacks such as the war on Iraq, even though it often had to proceed without the United States. Indeed, US unilateralism may have provoked a multilateral reaction in the rest of the world. The International Criminal Court and Kyoto Protocol on climate change went forward in the absence of the United States – and in the face of US hostility. Multilateralism carries the hopes of many around the globe looking for an alternative to hierarchy and force as a way of ordering the world. The multilateral instinct remains to try to introduce some order into a chaotic and anarchic world by prescribing heavy doses of government for the international system. The intention is to develop global political structure to the extent it can provide a match for and a complement to global economic integration, as well as curb collective insecurity and, in stronger versions, promote democracy, justice, and environmental conservation. The very fact that the system is international means that its government cannot be in the image of the sovereign nation-state; instead, government has to be constructed on a more piecemeal basis.

Multilateralism as Ongoing Project, and its Hazards

Multilateralism is not just a set of existing international institutions and their accomplishments. Rather, multilateralism is (in a way, like democracy) a continuing project. It is hard to imagine any liberal multilateralist looking at today's world and expressing satisfaction with what he or she sees.

There are of course positives in the record of these institutions since 1945. This is perhaps most apparent when it comes to the Bretton Woods financial system, which helped stave off the risk of global economic depression as experienced in the 1930s. The gradually more market-oriented successor regime to Bretton Woods retained many of its institutions, and continued to secure the international economy against global depression – though often at substantial cost to global equity. The United Nations for its part long had its peace-building potential impeded by the Cold War confrontation, and its successes are less obvious, but its defenders can point to, for example, peacekeeping operations, relief work, and the fostering of environmental agreements by the UN Environment Program.

Partial successes of existing global political arrangements notwithstanding, multilateralists would point to the work that needs to be done. Global environmental problems have barely begun to be addressed, despite being on the agenda for more than three decades (since at least the 1972 UN Conference on the Human Environment in Stockholm). The only episode that looks remotely like a success story is the 1987 Montreal Protocol for the protection of the ozone layer. There is no World Environment Organization at all comparable to the WTO to evaluate, anticipate, and respond to environmental threats. The climate change issue features glacial progress – the Kyoto Protocol of 1997 is the landmark, but when it came into force in 2005 it excluded the United States as well as emerging industrial giants China and India. Genocidal wars still happen. The proliferation of nuclear weapons and other "weapons of mass destruction" has not been brought under control. In the wake of 9/11 and the Iraq War, the world feels to most people a more insecure place (as indicated by opinion polls in many countries; see chapter 4) – and this feeling of insecurity has been intensified rather than alleviated by the US-directed "war on terror." International economic regimes are manifestly failing to reach those at the bottom of the global income distribution; most people in the Third World remain outside the global economy. Gaps between the world's poorest states and richer states continue to widen. Famines still happen in Third World countries. Authoritarian states and warlords in failed states continue to abuse human rights.

Liberal multilateralists believe that more needs to be done in terms of increasing both the scope and reach of multilateral institutions: scope in terms of the substantive policy areas they cover, reach in terms of the degree of control they can exercise in world affairs. They look especially to the European Union as a model for what can be accomplished. The EU achieves substantial restrictions on the sovereignty of its member states, making violent conflict between them impossible. It also regulates finance and commerce within Europe – most notably through the integration of its core members into a single currency. Increasingly it promotes Union-wide social and environmental policies.

Typically the negotiation of agreements that set up organizations or binding arrangements is a tortuous process involving representatives of nation-states. Painstaking negotiations usually culminate in the establishment of a body with no democratic features, but highly formalized allocations of responsibility and administrative rules. There is little transparency or accountability in the appointment of officials to run international organizations, especially if they are the product of career paths leading up through the organization in question. Such authority as sovereign states will agree to yield is typically handed over to unaccountable bureaucratic bodies operating at best in administrative fashion according to the constitutional mandate of the agreement that sets up the organization in question. The paradigm case here is perhaps the World Trade Organization, which is arguably quite effective in administering the international trade regime according to the precepts of neoliberal economics. But it took a decade of negotiations (the Uruguay Round of the GATT) to get to the point where the WTO was established.

135

The painstaking process through which they are established means that multilateral institutions are generally very heavy on formal rules for their operation. States signing up to these institutions know that there may be limited subsequent opportunities for renegotiation of the agreements that set them up (because renegotiation, like the original negotiations, is likely to be protracted and expensive). To the degree that there are opportunities for international institutions to take discretionary action, it is often exercised in practice by unelected and often unaccountable officials. I will now show why both constitutional and administrative excess lead to problem-solving deficiency. Identification of these limits is important because the kinds of institutions actually implemented as a result of the efforts of liberal multilateralists are especially prone to these two kinds of excess. Constitutional order and administrative structure do of course have their positive aspects, with plenty of achievements to look back upon. The trouble is that their application is subject to diminishing marginal net benefits as they try to extend their reach into increasingly complex problem areas, and eventually marginal net benefits turn negative. Let us see why.

First Problem for Multilateralists: Constitutional Excess

A constitution is a set of basic rules that specify the distribution of authority for making collective decisions, and the rights that individuals and other actors have against decision-makers (and against each other). Central to constitutionalization is limitation on arbitrary authority, which is why a constitution and the rule of law are often seen as central to liberal democratic states, protecting them against authoritarianism, securing freedom of speech, guarding private property, and otherwise promoting social safety, security, and prosperity. The more constitutionalized a system, the more it grants the legal system (in the form of a constitutional court or supreme court) the ultimate authority to pass judgment on the actions of other decision-makers (such as voters, administrators, parliaments, and presidents). In the absence of effective democratic control of the system, there is a danger that what Bohman (2004) calls "juridification" will lead to domination by the rules themselves.[3]

The international system is currently not heavily constitutionalized. Ikenberry (2001) refers to the post-World War II arrangements of Bretton Woods, the UN, and NATO as a constitutional order, but that is stretching a point. More important is the fact that contemporary multilateralists see the constitutionalization of the international system as their goal. Kersch (2004) describes a "global constitutional project." Held (2004: 111) proposes a "global constitutional convention" "involving states, IGOs, INGOs, citizen groups and social movements" joined in a "stakeholder process of consensus building." Archibugi (2004: 452) advocates the replacement of sovereignty by constitutionalism – that is, a constitutional structure that specifies the distribution of authority between all levels of government from the local to the global, policed by "juridical procedures." In practice, the European Union presents the most heavily constitutionalized international polity, and is often seen as the model. However, any problem-solving success in the EU can often be attributed to the multi-level networked governance that may occur in the vicinity of the constitutional framework of the EU, but not because of it, and sometimes despite it. EU rules are famously insensitive to variations in local conditions.

Excessive constitutionalization can be a problem, because the more rules there are, and the more fine-grained the rules in question, the more likely it is that any particular actor displeased with a decision will be able to find a constitutional rule that can be interpreted so as to support the grievance. However, it is also likely that those pleased with a decision will be able to find an interpretation of the same rule or a different one that will support their position. Constitutional excess means heavy demand on the legal system to be the ultimate arbiter when it comes to collective problem-solving. This is especially true in the United States, where most high-profile political disputes end up sooner or later in the courts for adjudication (foreign policy and national security policy are exceptions because they enjoy a large degree of constitutional exemption).

The more complex the situations that a constitutional order confronts, the harder it is for rules to apply to all contingencies. Specifying still more rules to compensate for the deficiencies of existing rules merely exacerbates the problem. An alternative response is to specify only procedural rules, and retreat from substance. For example, in US environmental policy, all major projects carried out or endorsed by the federal government come under the National Environmental Policy Act, which specifies that an environmental impact statement be prepared. But as interpreted by the courts, the Act requires only that an impact statement be prepared – not that environmental values be taken into account in governmental decision-making. Just about every environmental impact statement is the subject of legal challenge; but only on the basis of its intrinsic adequacy, which need bear no relation to decision-making. As a result, agencies preparing impact statements engage in overkill to ensure that impact statements pass muster, for which they can get approval from the courts in the absence of any link at all between impact statement and decision-making.

Constitutional engineering relies on a mechanistic view of the world. The idea is that people behave in predictable and invariant fashion. Good outcomes can then be achieved by devising a set of rules and institutions into which such people can be inserted. Designing a constitution is like designing a machine, with the components expected to perform consistently and predictably. Thus in the wake of the revolutions of 1989, it was assumed that provided the proper constitutional systems were put in place, market systems could flourish in post-communist countries. The consequences in some countries were not so bad, but the consequence in Russia was mafia capitalism. The Russian example shows that having the right constitution and legal rules in place is not enough to guarantee that the system works as intended, and that some alternative or supplementary source of order is necessary. That alternative might be a supportive discourse of the sort that did prove to exist in, say, Poland. Absent such a discourse, the obvious alternative is coercion. When it comes to Russia, the constitutional engineer would probably say that the real problem was that government could not or would not enforce private property rights effectively, such that the mafia stepped into the property-right-enforcement gap (Varese, 2001). Liberal constitutionalism in this case therefore requires a strong state. But the requisite strength cannot be specified or limited through purely constitutional means, because it is deficiency in such means that requires an increasingly strong state action to begin with. There is a temptation to keep on increasing the level of state coercion in the face of recalcitrant discourses and practices that do not fall into line in the way the constitutional blueprint requires (Dryzek 2004: 49). As the great conservative philosopher Edmund Burke put it more than 200 years ago in reflecting on the constitutional engineers of the French Revolution, "in the groves of their academy, at the end of every vista you see nothing but the gallows."

Now, it might be argued that the problem of constitutional excess hardly applies in an international system that is currently very weakly constitutionalized (except for the European Union), and does not have any strong system-level authority that might be tempted down the coercive path. But the problems I have identified would likely appear very quickly were the system to become more constitutionalized than it is at present. Standard constitutionalist accounts see the domination of formal rules (juridification) and over-centralization of authority as capable of rectification by vigilant citizens or their representatives who will if necessary rise to the defense of their republic. Bruce Ackerman (1991) points to occasions in United States history where this has happened (most recently, the New Deal in the 1930s). The global system is currently very short on cosmopolitan citizens or their representatives with this kind of civic commitment to the global polity. Even the European Union is lacking in this respect, as its peoples find it very hard to internalize any notion of citizenship beyond the state level.

There are many structures and processes that offer alternatives to constitutionalization in collective decision-making. But when it comes to multilateral institutional construction, the normal alternative has been to grant authority to some administrative body, such as the bureaucracy of the United Nations and its agencies, the IMF, World Bank, and WTO. But administrative rationalism is in the end no better at coping with the complexity attending globalization, for reasons I will now explain.

Second Problem for Multilateralists: Excessive Administration

The administrative and the constitutional impetus are different, because administrative rationalism assigns discretionary authority to administrators with responsibility for a particular problem (or sub-problem), while constitutionalism specifies the rules by which administrators must abide. Of course, it is possible to design systems that allow administrators freedom of action within constraints given by constitutional rules.

Excessive administration is a problem because truly complex problems of the kind that abound in today's globalizing world impose stress on bureaucratic forms of organization and the instrumental-analytic notion of rationality that underpins bureaucracy. Interdependence and interconnectedness are defining features of globalization (Held and McGrew, 2000: 1), but they also help define the concept of complexity. Thus globalization means actors face increasing complexity, almost at the level of definition. Complexity exists to the extent of the number and variety of elements and interactions in the environment of a decision process, be it a human brain, a government, or a social movement.

Bureaucracy exemplifies the instrumental-analytical approach to rationality that pretty much defined the modern era. "Instrumental" means goal-directed. "Analysis" means, quite literally, breaking down a complex problem into its parts in order to apprehend and solve it. Administrative structures respond to complexity by disaggregating complex problems into their component parts. Each component is then assigned to a problem-solving unit to deal with in isolation. Once each unit has crafted its response, then these responses can be aggregated into overall solutions responsive to all the facets of a complex problem. This is the approach to problem-solving described a century ago by Max Weber in his classic account of bureaucracy. For Weber, bureaucracy was the supremely rational and modern form of organization precisely because it could cope with complexity. Disaggregation of complex problems is the rationale for the familiar organization chart of a bureaucracy – hierarchical and pyramid shaped. And bureaucracies have indeed proved quite successful when it comes to coping with moderate degrees of complexity. Examples might include organizing production in a factory, organizing courses, students, and instructors into classroom spaces in a university, running a social insurance system, even fighting a war. Of course, bureaucracies are not perfect when it comes to such tasks, and they are attacked from all parts of the political spectrum for their failings. But there is no denying the number of things they can do when faced with complex problems (which is not to say they are necessarily ever the best means for dealing with any given level of complexity).

Why then do systems grounded in instrumental-analytical rationality eventually fail when confronted with growing complexity? Their main difficulty stems from the fact that to be effective, problem disaggregation must be intelligent. The main organizing principle here is that interactions across the boundaries of the subsets into which the complex problem has been subdivided must be relatively sparse, while interactions within subsets are relatively dense (Simon, 1981). But as complexity increases, then so by definition do the number and variety of interactions across any conceivable division of problem-solving labor that defines the sets and sub-sets. Each sub-unit will take actions that make sense from the point of view of its own narrow remit, but have largely negative consequences for other sub-units. Take the WTO, which has been quite successful in pursuing the economic mandate that set it up. However, WTO decisions also have enormous implications when it comes to issues of global justice and environmental conservation, among other non-economic values; but any such values are routinely subordinated to the economic mandate of the WTO when they are not ignored completely. The 2002 *National Security Strategy of the United States of America* treats economic integration as a challenge to national security (suggesting the possibility of a clash between US unilateralism and the world trade regime), driving home the connection between economic and non-economic values.

Eventually, the analytical intelligence and cognitive capacities that coordinate the system as a whole become stressed, and at some point break down completely. With time, we see not convergence on some less problematical conditions, but rather endless displacement of difficulties across the boundaries of sets and subsets (Dryzek, 1987b; for an application to ecological problems, see Dryzek 1987a). Just when stress leading to breakdown occurs is an empirical matter. Critics of central planning from F. A. von Hayek (1979) to Christopher Alexander (1965) to James C. Scott (1998) and beyond have argued that the breakdown comes rather quickly. In support, they can point to many examples of failure. These include the inability of Soviet-style planned economies to produce consumer goods that people actually wanted, the disastrous effects of centralized city planning on the conviviality of urban life, the failure of large-scale social engineering of the sort attempted in President Johnson's "War on Poverty" in the 1960s, and the inability of the US intelligence services to piece together the bits of information in their possession that would have revealed the plot to attack the World Trade Center and Pentagon on September 11, 2001.[4]

It is widely recognized that their overwhelmingly administrative character means that existing multilateral arrangements suffer from a massive democratic deficit.

Archibugi (2004: 459–60) recognizes "the dangers of a global technocracy" (while hoping it can be remedied by "more accountability and transparency within the international organizations"). As Higgott (2004: 7) puts it, "the top down global governance agenda of the late 1990s and early 21st century is still driven by an understanding of governance as *effectiveness* and *efficiency*, not governance as greater representation, accountability, and justice." What is less often noticed is that this democratic deficit also entails a rationality deficit, because there are limits to the degree to which unaccountable administration can make rational decisions without openness to telling criticism from a variety of perspectives that democracy enables (see the classic statement of Popper, 1966).

Governments and organizations can try to overcome some of the pathologies of constitutional and administrative excess to the degree their problem-solving is networked, as described in chapter 5. Multilateralism does not necessarily oppose the growth of networked governance. Indeed, the two could be cast as allies against US attempts to assert control over the international system, for networks too can evade hegemony (be they networks of terrorists or of financial institutions and corporations). But effective networks generally arise from the bottom up in what Hayek (1979) would call a spontaneous order (like the market), whereas multilateralists are more interested in top-down negotiated order.

Multilateralism Confronts Reflexive Modernization

The kind of reflexive modernization discussed in chapter 6 also causes problems for the multilateral project. Reflexive modernization means that the ratio of questioning to obedience increases in relation to the traditions into which people are socialized. Constitutional thinking is actually consistent with what Beck (1992) calls "semi-modernity," where people behave in predictable and consistent ways once inserted into a constitutional structure. If individuals do not treat constitutional rules as "natural," then constitutions may find themselves without the kind of supportive discourse necessary to make them work. Reflexive modernization means that rules and discourses alike lose their grip on behavior, and instead become more amenable to questioning and rethinking. However, all this is a matter of degree, for such questioning itself can only be situated within the "discursive field" (Bourdieu, 1993) in which questioners are located, and helps to constitute who they are.

Here a tension arises between constitutionalization and democracy. Constitutionalism requires that people behave in predictable ways and accept the constitutional order as quasi-natural. Democracy requires autonomy on the part of citizens. In a reflexive modernity, that consists in part of the capacity to call into question traditions and discourses, in a way that might prove to undermine constitutional order. This is not to say that constitutionalism should be rejected, simply that the more a system of governance becomes heavily constitutionalized, the more it presents problems for democracy.[5] This tension lies at the heart of the project of cosmopolitan democracy in particular (which I will discuss in more detail in the next chapter), given that its design for the international system is so heavily constitutional. The cosmopolitan and democratic aspects of the project may pull in different directions. This tension may not yet be apparent in the real world, given the shortage of cosmopolitan institutions in the contemporary international system. It would show up with any success of the cosmopolitan project

It remains ironic that at the very moment administrative and constitutionalized problem-solving seem to be yielding to networked governance at national, regional, and local levels, liberal multilateralists still seek to risk replicating these questionable models at the global level. It is doubly ironic given that the reasons for the shift from administrative and constitutionalized models to more informal networked governance appear to apply very strongly at the global level: notably, complexity and the incidence of novel problems defying clear demarcations of problem-solving responsibility. Increasing reflexive awareness on the part of individuals, groups, and movements that no longer accept the traditions in which they have been socialized (including traditions that specify uncritical acceptance of constitutional precepts) can be found at all levels, from the local to the global. At the global level, anticorporate globalization movements beginning in the late 1990s can be interpreted in terms of growing reflexive awareness. In the previous chapter I showed how resistance can sometimes play key roles in reordering the world by discursive means. A strongly constitutional liberal multilateralist program of institutional construction sits uneasily in a world where multiple and contested discourses are important. Sometimes hegemonic discourses might stabilize particular constitutional arrangements, but that is increasingly rare.

Conclusion

Inasmuch as liberal multilateralism emphasizes the specification of constitutional rules and the design of administrative structures, it ignores the presence of discourses, and in particular contending discourses. It may be that a particular multilateral institution can find a hegemonic discourse in order to stabilize it and make it work. Such was the case with the Bretton Woods institutions, and more recently the WTO, whose effectiveness would scarcely be imaginable were it not for the weight of key actors in the international economy who have internalized market liberal discourse. However, it may also be the case that a particular institution is undermined by competing discourses. The global free trade regime may be undermined by the discourse of counter-terror, to the extent that the free movement of goods becomes seen as a security threat. International institutions for the protection of human rights (such as the Geneva Convention) may also be undermined by the discourse of counter-terror. The International Court of Justice in The Hague, notionally the judicial arm of the United Nations, has become an irrelevance because it cannot find a supportive discourse; and cannot assert itself against strong conceptions of national sovereignty. Market liberalism itself can be disruptive when it comes to institutions that are initially non-economic. For example, multilateral negotiations on institutions for the promotion of sustainable development at the 2002 World Summit on Sustainable Development ran headlong into a presumption of the dominance of economic ways of thinking on the part of negotiators from the US and its supporters committed to market liberalism. Such discourse contests are beneath the radar of multilateralists preoccupied with the formal aspects of institutional design.

Liberal multilateralism's heart is in the right place, most clearly in its pursuit of international peace and cooperation, more controversially when it comes to economic affairs. Its appeal is unsurprisingly strong to those appalled by the unilateral policies of the United States, especially when directed by neoconservative ideology, and seeking an alternative way to order international affairs. Its attractions increase to the degree any cosmopolitan democratic twist can be added to it. But in a complex world that features competing discourses as opposed to formal rules and strategic interactions, its prospects are a bit dubious. All this is not to say that liberal multilateralism and cosmopolitan ideals should be abandoned, but rather that any such projects should be mindful of their own limits to the degree they remain formalistic and so prone to excessive constitionalization and administrative rationalism.

In the next chapter I will discuss the efforts of cosmopolitan democrats to devise institutions that have more in the way of democratic control. A cosmopolitan democrat would say that the whole point is to create international organizations that are not like the WTO or UN, that are instead directly accountable to the citizenry of the world. But if so, the cosmopolitan has to show exactly how multilateral negotiations can produce flexible and democratic institutional arrangements of a kind they have never produced in the past. If the cosmopolitan cannot so demonstrate this possibility, then liberal multilateralism is likely only to produce more heavily constitutionalized and highly administered systems of government of precisely the kind that now seems so problematic in the affairs of government at all levels – and which is yielding to networked governance.

Multilateralists should, then, bear in mind the degree to which the world features multiple contested discourses, where politics (especially democratic politics) is in large matter a question of their engagement. If this is ignored, multilateralism risks sapping the discursive and democratic energy of international political life.

8

Three Kinds of Democracy

Recent years have seen increasing interest in extending democracy into an international system long inhospitable to democratic projects beyond the level of the nation-state. The basic justification is that systems and institutions of global governance have become increasingly consequential, and that just like any system of governance their legitimacy ought to rest on democratic principles (Patomäki, 2003: 348). Rationality as problem-solving effectiveness is at issue too, as well as peace and social justice, and democracy can have substantial positive implications for these values. But democracy, and in particular the project of advancing democracy, can mean radically different things. In this chapter I will contrast the discursive approach with two other prominent models: the neoconservatism that came to prominence in the declared mission of the US government to bring democracy to ever more parts of the world, and the cosmopolitan democracy that constitutes the strongest and most ambitious version of liberal multilateralism.

Neoconservative Democratization

Neoconservatives want to spread democracy in the world. In keeping with Fukuyama's (1989, 1992) "end of history" thesis, they believe that there is only one successful political and economic model that is universally applicable to all societies, not just to Western ones. In the words of the first sentence of the 2002 *National Security Strategy of the United States of America*, there is a "single sustainable model for national success: freedom, democracy, and free enterprise." Once states recognize this, they can participate fully in the world economic system, and also the community of democratic states that do not wage war on each other – the "democratic peace" thesis. While their opponents outside the US see this as thin cover for imperialist adventures, the neoconservatives deserve the benefit of the doubt: they are genuinely committed to democracy, or at least democracy as they understand it. However, there are several problems with their democratization project.

The first is that it conceptualizes democracy in wholly American terms: as going hand-in-hand with capitalist markets and the institutions that support such markets. States are judged democratic or not by the United States, so Iran is defined outside the democratic orbit despite its competitive elections. In neoconservative democratization, the will of the people is to be expressed only through elections that are competitive, but do not allow for the victory of (say) anti-capitalist or anti-Western fundamentalists. The idea that elections can be problematic in divided societies, especially if the electoral rules are not written exactly right (so as to encourage moderate behavior by party leaders) simply does not register. Nor do the constraints that capitalism imposes on democracy. While capitalist economic development may facilitate the creation of a minimal liberal democracy (in part by creating a working class with a vested interest in democracy; see Rueschemeyer et al., 1992), capitalism also imposes strict limits on the kinds of policies that governments can choose. This is especially true to the degree a state is integrated into the international economic system (see the discussion of globalization in chapter 5). Not only is the neoconservative model of democracy made in America, it is perceived as such by those on the receiving end of attempts to impose it – and meets resistance for that very reason.

The second problem is inconsistency between means and ends. Neoconservatives want to impose democracy if necessary at the point of a gun, as in Iraq. There is no possibility for ordinary people to participate in their own democratization project – except to play the roles assigned to them by the American authors of their democracy. The gamble is that people will accept these roles. But democracy is about the capacity of people to author their own collective destiny – not simply to act out a script written in the United States. Neoconservatives would respond that US intervention in Iraq was followed by a 2005 election in which most eligible Iraqis participated, and by demands elsewhere in the Arab world for more popularly accountable government. But causal inference is difficult when it comes to other Arab countries; those pressing for greater democracy certainly did not wish to be associated with the United States and its actions in Iraq.

But from the point of view of transnational democratization, the third and most significant defect of the neoconservative approach is that it conceptualizes democracy only as an attribute of nation-states. The idea that democracy might enter the international system in relations between or across states is treated with scorn. Neoconservatives support unilateral action to impose American values that are at the same time supposed to be universal values. There is no scope for democratic negotiation across or within states, even allied states, as to what these values might mean – let alone that accepts they may not be as universal as neoconservatives believe. Order in the international system is to be dictated by the benign superpower, the United States. Thus, as we ascend levels of political organization, there is a knife edge between enthusiasm for (a particular kind of) democracy at the level of the nation-state, and hostility to democracy at any level above or across the nation-state. Neoconservatives are hostile to international institutions (especially the United Nations) that do not follow American prescriptions. And the idea that international institutions might claim legitimacy through their democratic character, and so challenge US sovereignty, is anathema.

Thus in the end neoconservatism cannot speak to democratization of the international system itself, other than to oppose it. Neoconservatism is not designed for a world that is populated by reflexive actors, and ordered by networks and discourses rather than formal organizations and their interactions. It fails the test of reflexivity, inasmuch as it stands outside the world as constituted by discourses, believing that this world can be engineered from the outside. This may help to explain why it appears so unacceptable outside the United States, and as such plays no part as a cross-nationally ordering discourse in international affairs. Though ultimately seeking a reordered and more peaceful international system, its role in the international system we currently have is disruptive.

Cosmopolitan Democratization

In contrast to neoconservative democratization, the project of cosmopolitan democracy is committed to the creation of democratic international institutions. Though allowing an ancillary role for group activity in transnational civil society, cosmopolitanism emphasizes the construction of formal institutions, especially governmental organizations and legal systems. Cosmopolitan democracy favors an international system more densely populated by institutions that both secure order and are democratically accountable in direct fashion – that is, not just at one remove, through any accountability of states that take part in such arrangements (Archibugi and Held, 1995; Held, 1995; Archibugi et al., 1998). Such institutions might include to begin with more regional bodies like the EU, a UN Security Council that is more inclusive and effective, international courts (such as the International Criminal Court), cross-national referenda, and international military authorities. Institutions would exist at multiple levels, not necessarily subordinate to higher levels as in a federal system. They would however be subject to a common legal framework, "a system of diverse and overlapping power centres shaped by democratic law" (Held, 1995: 234). The project looks forward ultimately to an international legal system enforcing democratically determined laws, a global parliament to hold all other global institutions to account, and international control of a military that would in the long run yield demilitarization (cosmopolitans can accept the distant and utopian character of these latter aspirations).[1] The project is distinguished by "its attachment to the centrality of the rule of law and constitutionalism as necessary conditions for the establishment of a more democratic world order" (McGrew, 2002: 276). David Held, the most prominent cosmopolitan democrat, also anticipates an interventionist and transnationally social-democratic economic policy, matching economic globalization with "global social integration and a commitment to social justice" under the auspices of cosmopolitan institutions (Held, 2004: 56).

Cosmopolitanism was set on the back foot in the aftermath of the terrorist attacks of September 11, 2001, and in particular by a superpower bent on unilateral action in a number of arenas, undermining the multilateral basis of cosmopolitan democracy. While US unilateralism did provoke some multilateral reaction in the rest of the world, a cosmopolitan democratic project with the sole remaining superpower standing both outside and hostile would be very different from the kind of world sought by cosmopolitans themselves. Under President George W. Bush the United States declared a right to identify and classify actual and potential enemies around the globe, and to undertake whatever action it saw fit in order to subordinate them. International institutions were scorned if they fail to fall in line with US wishes; prior to the invasion of Iraq, the UN was asked by Bush to demonstrate its relevance by approving US action. When it did not, it was brushed aside. In addition, the US consistently opposed key aspects of the multilateral project such as the International Criminal Court, the Kyoto Protocol, and other international efforts aimed at environmental protection.

The multilateral project can still limp along in the face of US hostility. But if it were ever to stop limping and start galloping, it would run headlong into the pathologies of constitutional and administrative excess that I identified in chapter 7. A cosmopolitan political order would be highly constitutionalized, with formal rules arrived at through painstaking negotiation (and the more divided the world, the more painstaking the negotiation has to be). Where the rules stop, administration begins; and the standard hierarchical kind of administration is, as I have argued in chapter 7, problematic in a complex and fluid world. The international system is in fact evolving into a very different kind of networked governance, held together by the glue of discourses, that liberal multilateralism and cosmopolitanism would seek to supplant with more formal organization at the system level.

Cosmopolitanism rests uneasily in a divided world. Its basic premise is that individuals everywhere could come to see themselves as citizens of the world, and so consent to the subordination of their national, regional, tribal, religious, and civilizational identities to this common project. Throughout the world, identity politics is pervasive and has been growing since the end of the Cold War; and the identity in question is never global. Other divisions pit "civilizations" against one another – or, rather, as I have argued in chapter 2, particular discourses that appear civilizational are constructed in opposition to one another. "Wars of ideas" are mobilized. The forces of global capitalism face all kinds of local resistances that coalesce into opposition to corporate globalization. Divisions have been raised not just between the US and its obvious enemies (such as Islamic radicals), but also between the US and its erstwhile allies in Europe and elsewhere, between the dominant superpower and anti-war movements around the globe. Within the United States, there is a strong belief in the universality of American ideals of democracy and freedom. However, the idea that they could ever be negotiable in light of non-American conceptions of democracy and freedom (let alone equality and distributive justice) is rejected across pretty much all of the American political spectrum.

In short, a divided world of discourse contestation causes problems for the cosmopolitan project. Even if the project could be renewed by overcoming US unilateralism, the kind of divided world it faces means that its formal institutions would have to be constructed in painstaking multilateral negotiations in an environment of deep difference. Thus even were these negotiations to produce formal institutions of the strength and reach desired by cosmopolitans, there is no defense against the hazards of constitutional and administrative excess identified in chapter 7. The cosmopolitan hope for more democratic and flexible global institutions is just that – a hope.

Discursive Democratization

The kind of democracy I have been arguing for throughout is transnational and discursive, highlighting dispersed and competent control over the engagement of discourses in transnational public spheres, which in turn constructs or influences international outcomes in a variety of ways. Transnational democracy of this sort is not electoral democracy, and it is not institutionalized in formal organizations. Instead, it is to be sought in communicatively competent decentralized control over the content and relative weight of globally consequential discourses, which in turn resonates with theories of deliberative democracy stressing communicative action in the public sphere (Chambers, 2003; Dryzek, 2000). The public sphere encompasses social movements and media communications, and can reach into corporations, states, and intergovernmental organizations. It is an informal, communicative realm that can be contrasted with the constitutional exercise of authority (though it can of course influence the latter).

One could argue the case for such democratization on purely normative grounds, but any such case would only have real-world bite to the extent it can build upon existing discourse aspects of international affairs. I have argued that

154

conflicts in the contemporary international system can most persuasively be interpreted in terms of the clash of discourses. Recognition of the importance of this dimension opens up possibilities for dispersed and competent control over the engagement of discourses – deliberative global politics. Discourses cannot be governed, but they can be engaged. I have argued not just for the intrinsic merits of such an approach (through reference to democratic values), but also for its effectiveness in achieving reconciliation across division, social justice, and generally helping to resolve social problems. Denial of the discourse dimension makes intelligent action in the system impossible. The democratic question then becomes how dispersed, critical, and competent influence over this contestation can be promoted, bearing in mind that decentralization does not necessarily equal democracy, that particular discourses can take oppressive and constraining form, and that interventions in the world of discourses can be designed to manipulate and control them.

Diffuse and decentralized control does not of itself signal democracy. Perfect markets are decentralized but not democratic, because they produce results based on the operation of economic mechanisms in which money alone matters, not political ones where public voice is possible. Perfect Hobbesian anarchy is also decentralized but not democratic, because its results are based on the balance of threat, coercion, and sometimes violence. Decentralized networked governance does not have to be democratic. For as pointed out in chapter 5, the replacement of centralized hierarchies by networks may actually mean a reduction in democratic accountability, because in networks it is often not clear where power actually lies, and so it is hard to hold those who wield power accountable for their actions. At least in hierarchies it is clear who holds ultimate power (at least formally), even if it can be hard to bring them to account. Decentralized control is only democratic to the degree it involves communicative action engaged by critical and competent individuals, acting as citizens and not as consumers, enemies, or automatons.

Particular discourses can themselves take on oppressive

and constraining form. Followers of Michel Foucault point to the degree to which people apparently acting freely may in truth be under the sway of dominant and oppressive discourses. These discourses may feature the assertion of identities that can only be validated through denial of competing identities – be they ethnic, religious, nationalistic, or "civilizational." Foucault himself pointed to the "governmentality" that accompanies liberal government in the modern world. In this light, liberalism creates subjects in ways that make them amenable and pliant when it comes to their place in the liberal political economy. These individuals apparently possess all kinds of rights but are in truth capable of interpreting them and exercising them only in ways that do not challenge the structure of the system.

More concerted and conscious manipulation is carried out by those who recognize the importance of the discourse dimension of international politics, but seek to bend it more to their liking. I have discussed "war of ideas" and "soft power" in this light (see chapter 4), but spin, public relations, and propaganda can also play their parts.

These three challenges of decentralized yet undemocratic authority, oppressive discourses, and discourse manipulation simply indicate that transnational discursive democracy, in common with any other democratization project, faces an uphill struggle in the contemporary international system. I have tried to show in earlier chapters how these sorts of difficulties can be recognized and countered. So while decentralization does not have to be democratic, the scarcity of centralized authority in the international system is one less obstacle to discursive democratization (chapter 5). Deliberation in transnational public spheres, diffuse reflexive action on the part of political actors, social movements resisting war and corporate globalization, issue-specific governance networks all have parts to play here. Indeed, they have much more important roles to play when it comes to international politics than they do in domestic politics within states, because in the international system formal sources of authority, let alone democratic authority, are weak. In today's more reflexive world, it is harder for oppressive discourses to take effect beneath the conscious awareness of subjects (chapter 6). Reflexive modernization means actors are increasingly likely to question discourses, rather than accept them. And wars of ideas, soft power, propaganda, and spin are hard to sustain in a world where globalizing communications can make it very difficult for those who try to segment and control different audiences (chapter 4).

In principle, the discursive emphasis has always been more feasible than the cosmopolitan project because the latter requires two steps: first, the establishment of stronger system-level institutions, and second, their democratization. Transnational discursive democracy, in contrast, requires only one step: the democratization of existing discourse-related sources of order. In the post-9/11 and post-Iraq world, the more informal discursive approach has enhanced plausibility in comparison to the formal apparatus central to the cosmo-politan model – though both are troubled by more centralized and hierarchical responses to international insecu-rity. The normative commitments of transnational democracy of any type are attacked by unilateralists contemptuous of international public opinion (Kaldor, 2003: 148).

The example of the impact of the anti-corporate globaliza-tion movement on international economic institutions (see chapter 6) might suggest that transnational discursive democ-racy succeeds to the extent it renders international institutions such as the World Bank, IMF, and WTO more directly accountable to the global citizenry and therefore more truly cosmopolitan, illustration of the complementary character of these two democratic projects. However, such an interpretation would not be on target. For transnational dis-cursive democracy can take effect in the absence of any formal international institutions simply by affecting the deci-sions of states with the capacity to make authoritative decisions within their jurisdictions, corporations, and the dif-fuse governance mechanisms stressed by Rosenau and Czempiel (1992). For example, international public spheres associated with the rights of indigenous peoples, global justice, or opposition to biopiracy are influential mainly when it comes to affecting the policies of states and corporations. Claims for transnational discursive democracy would stand even in the absence of any formal international institutions. Transnational discursive democracy is not, then, just another twist to liberal multilateralism, for it does not rest on the constitutionalization of the international system. This is not to ignore the continuing importance of formal international organizations and formal state organizations in producing authoritative decisions. But the limits of democratization of such formal organizations may have been reached; in which case the future of democracy is to be sought in the more informal realm that I have identified.

From Models of Democratic Government to Processes of Democratic Governance

Those versed in democracy as it applies within the sovereign state might point to the radical incompleteness of transnational discursive democracy on the grounds that it seems to deal only in influence, and not authority. Such democratic traditionalists could more easily look upon cosmopolitan democracy with approval, on the grounds that it has recognizable centers of decision-making authority in the form of international courts, legislatures, and administrative structures. Cosmopolitan democracy looks forward to a world where such formal institutions are established, even though they exist only weakly at the moment. Cosmopolitan democracy is, in short, a model of democracy.

The kind of transnational discursive democracy sketched here, in contrast, lacks formalized connection to binding collective decisions; the *sine qua non* of democracy defined literally as "the rule of the people." And in the absence of such mechanisms, traditionalists might argue that one should not speak of democracy at all. Walzer (1996) argues that one should not even speak of citizenship (let alone democracy) in settings that deny individuals the possibility to participate formally in collective decision-making. Such an argument would cut off the discursive practices I have described from democracy; though if it does, the fault lies not in the practices themselves, but rather in the recalcitrant undemocratic character of existing transnational institutions. But wherever the fault lies, transnational discursive democracy is not, it seems, a model of democracy.

This feature can however be made to work for discursive democracy rather than against it. Models of democracy are ideal types. When that ideal is close to existing practice, the model often works as an apology for the status quo. Such is the case most notably for models of pluralism and polyarchy developed by US political scientists such as David Truman (1951) and Robert Dahl (1956), which were essentially idealized pictures of US politics. When the ideal is far from existing practice, then it has a utopian aspect. Such is the case for cosmopolitan democracy. Utopian models can be helpful, especially when it comes to highlighting flawed aspects of the status quo. But they always beg the question of how to get from here to there. In addition, they beg the question of what happens when we get "there" – in the unlikely event we ever do; human history is generally not like this.

Utopian blueprints cannot easily be implemented in democratic fashion. In complex human social and political systems, something will always go wrong in the implementation. When things do, there is always a temptation to resort to just a little bit of coercion to put matters right. Popper (1966) argues that the normal fate of utopian social engineering is dictatorship, irrespective of the intentions of the engineers. Popper himself had communist and fascist schemes in mind, but the criticism is equally applicable to (say) free market utopias. The economic model specified in the Washington Consensus long administered by the IMF and (less assiduously) the World Bank has never been accepted by democratic majorities in countries on the receiving end of the medicine. Reluctant governments (no matter how they came to power) have generally imposed this medicine on reluctant peoples.

Proponents of the cosmopolitan model would protest that it is not utopian in this sense, that it merely seeks to build upon and extend existing features of the international system. These existing features would include a core of liberal democratic states, regional institutions such as the European Union, international law, the United Nations and its agencies, and norms such as universal human rights. Yet it would be just as easy to list features that obstruct the cosmopolitan vision. These obstructive features would include non-Western opposition to liberal precepts (and capitalist precepts), norms of sovereignty, militarization, the global arms trade and its vested interests, US unilateralism, the undemocratic character of international economic organizations under sway of market liberal economic doctrine, the reluctance of wealthy states to cede any power to poorer states, the sheer complexity and variety of governance mechanisms in international politics, defying easy subsumption under any grand centralizing logic. What exactly is to be done about all of these obstructive features if cosmopolitan institutional innovation is derailed by them? Popper's cautions about the implementation of blueprints might still be relevant here.

While it is a radical project, transnational discursive democratization does not anticipate any well-defined model of democracy radically different from the status quo, and so is immune to such temptations. It is actually much more useful here to think in terms of processes of democratization, rather than models of democracy (Dryzek, 1996: 4–6). Such processes can begin from any point, most straightforwardly the status quo in any particular political system, such as the contemporary international system. The idea then is to figure out how the sources of authority and governance mechanisms that actually and already exist in that system can be democratized. Such democratization can itself be reflexive and democratic, a process engaged by many actors.

Discursive democratization in any situation means more effective inclusion of different voices, bringing an increasing range of questions to the public agenda, and rendering communication and deliberation more open and less prone

160

to symbolic distortion. (In Dryzek 1996: 5–9 these three dimensions are labeled respectively franchise, scope, and authenticity.) The concern is always with the democratization of systems as they currently exist.

The international system as it currently exists is characterized by a vast array of governance mechanisms, ranging from the highly formalized to the completely informal. They include international organizations, markets, regimes, treaties, international laws, norms, tacit bargains, military force, coercive diplomacy, non-governmental organizations, private governance, civil society regulation, transgovernmental arrangements, confederations of states, and public spheres. In light of this complexity, it is more practical to think of the democratization of particular mechanisms that do exist rather than their subordination to some grand institution-building logic. It is in complex situations that such grand logic is likely to go astray (or become coercive). The kind of democratization I have emphasized is discursive, because in all of these governance mechanisms contending discourses are likely to be at issue. The main difference between the international system and the political systems inside sovereign states is the relative informality and variety of governance mechanisms in the former, which is why discourses play a comparatively greater role in producing and coordinating outcomes than in domestic politics. Democratic governance in the international system must then look very different from democratic government within states. It *is* democracy, Jim – but not as we know it.

Faces of Power and Sites of Democracy

We can drive home this contrast between domestic and international politics by examining the kinds of power prevalent in each. There are four main kinds of power. The first is the most overt and straightforward, revealed when A makes B do something that B does not wish to do, with some explicit penalty for non-compliance on B's part (Dahl, 1963). The second face is slightly more subtle, consisting of A's manipulation of decision processes to make sure that A's and not B's interests prevail (Bachrach and Baratz, 1962). The third face exists when B perceives its own interests in such a way as to suit A; in this case, B will not even be aware that power is being exercised (Lukes, 1974). (For example, feminists would argue that women have often misperceived their own interests in ways that suit males.) A fourth kind of power is embedded in shared understandings that define who actors are, what motives they have, what entities exist in their world, what sorts of relationships between actors are natural and unnatural. This fourth type is the "disciplinary power" highlighted by Foucault (1980) and others; it is constituted in discourses. To Foucault, discourses are often hegemonic and hold individuals in an iron grip of which they are completely unaware. I have argued that the contemporary international system generally features discourse contestation rather than discourse hegemony. It is in the third and fourth types of power that identities get defined; and in a divided world, the politics of identity is especially pressing.

Democracy means that *whatever* kind of power exists should be subject to dispersed and competent control by the relevant citizenry. Most democratic theorists are most comfortable operating within the context provided by the domestic politics of the sovereign state. Many such theories recognize only the first two types of power, and it is a straightforward matter to seek their democratization via the appropriate constitutional rules that specify how collective decisions shall be made, what capacities people have to help make them (for example, through elections), and the protections that individuals ought to have against arbitrary exercise of power.

But even in domestic politics, democratic constitutional design will often leave the third and fourth kinds of power untouched – and that is why, for example, democratic theory has had so much trouble in coping with the politics of identity, or the power exercised by business elites. Corporate advertising, propaganda, and spin-doctoring may combine to convince people that their political interests are the same as those of some elite; for example, that they have an interest in an unequal distribution of income, or dubious wars. Dominant discourses may constrain the way people conceptualize the world – for example, in mobilizing ethnic or national identities in resentful and murderous form.

Thus to the degree order and conflict in domestic politics stem from hegemonic or contending discourses, discursive democracy interpreted as dispersed and competent control over the engagement of discourses becomes central to democratization of the system. When it comes to transnational politics, order and conflict are still more a matter of either hegemonic or contending discourses than in domestic politics. The first two sorts of power are not absent in the international system. But the capacity of any actor A to influence actor B to do something in A's interests by using threat of sanction (the first type of power) is diminished by the relative absence of coercive authorities backed by law of the sort that we find in domestic politics. Of course, this sort of power still exists in the international system, as "realists" whose view of the system highlights power based on the threat of violence by states against each other would be the first to remind us (see chapter 1), and neoconservatives put their faith in this kind of power. But most of the time, most transnational interaction is not composed of threats. What this means is that the relative importance of the third and fourth types of power is stronger in transnational than in domestic politics. And thus discursive democratization is especially promising as an orientation to democratization at the international level. Conventional democratic theory (including cosmopolitan theory) is much more at home in a world where the first two types of power predominate, because then formal institutional design is the main task. But this is a very different world from the contemporary international system.

Thus the case for discursive democracy can be made not just in terms of the intrinsic attractiveness of competing normative approaches, but also in terms of the way the world actually works, and what is feasible within it. I began in chapter 1 by arguing that many of the more important sources of division in today's world are grounded in competing discourses; and that such competition certainly captures what is going on in the international system better than alleged hegemony on the part of any particular discourse. The divisions in question include alleged clashes of civilizations, identity conflicts in divided societies, war on terror, counter-terror versus human rights, corporate globalization against localized and networked resistance, militarized unilateralism versus anti-war movements, and promethean industrialism against sustainable development.

These sorts of divisions cannot readily be governed on a top-down basis – and any such attempt is itself likely to generate discourses of resistance. But divisions across discourses can be engaged. Divisions that are constituted by discourses can also be negotiated through discursive means. Such engagement can be the essence of deliberative and democratic global politics.

Notes

1 More formally, any discourse will normally contain:

   i An *ontology*. That is, key entities whose existence is recognized or denied. Such entities might include God, individuals, social classes, or nations.

   ii *Agents*. Some of these entities will be recognized as having the capacity to act, others treated as only capable of being acted upon. For example, traditional realist discourse in international relations emphasizes states as the key agents, ignoring (say) NGOs and transnational corporations. Marxists, in contrast, would see social classes as the key agents, with the state the instrument of the dominant class (at least in crude Marxism).

   iii *Motives*. Agents can be seen as moved by self-interest, perhaps in narrow material terms, or by concern for some common good. Economic discourses assume material self-interest as the universal motivation, realism assumes states maximize security.

   iv *Natural relationships*. Particular sorts of relationships may be regarded as natural or unnatural. So market liberals regard competition as natural. Realists regard violent conflict as part of the natural order. Feminists would stress more empathetic and cooperative relationships.

Other possibilities here include equality, cooperation, and hierarchies based on race, gender, wealth, or intelligence.

v *Metaphors and other rhetorical devices*. Metaphors might include the idea that states interact like billiard balls on a table (popular in potted descriptions of realism), the idea that the earth is like a "spaceship" in its fragile life support systems (once popular in environmentalism), or that international affairs are like a Western movie (in President Ronald Reagan's view of foreign policy). Other rhetorical devices include horror stories about adversaries, appeals to quasi-religious images about the destiny of one's cause, or invocations of some imagined past golden age.

2 Hajer (1993) speaks of "discourse coalitions" of actors.

3 Hegemony in this sense was first used by the Italian theorist Antonio Gramsci in the 1920s to explain the acceptance of capitalist values as universal values by many workers whom he thought should otherwise be rebelling against capitalism.

4 That conception may apply differentially within the system. Keene (2002) points out that modern sovereignty norms only ever applied to Western states, with colonial norms in operation for the rest of the world. And as Krasner (1999) shows, modern sovereignty has never been absolute. These sorts of qualifications do not change the hegemonic character of sovereignty norms. Reus-Smit (1999: 164–5) allows that contemporary developments concerning the spread of human rights norms, market liberalization, environmentalism, regionalism, and networks of intergovernmental and non-governmental organizations may change what sovereignty means, but "the long term effect of these factors is unclear" (p. 165).

5 One of the most important assets a transnational corporation possesses is its brand, increasingly recognized by accountants and markets as an asset that can have millions of dollars attached to it – independent of the material assets that a company also possesses. Public perceptions of a brand exist entirely in the symbolic realm, and the brand itself can become a site of political contestation as activists challenge perceived corporate misbehavior.

6   International relations scholars are careful to distinguish the neorealism of Waltz from the classical realism of Morgenthau (1985) and others. These are indeed different theories, the former grounding its explanations in the anarchical structure of the international system, the latter in assumptions about the power-maximizing character of state leaders. Their evaluations vary: neorealists believe a bipolar system is most stable (because anarchy is attenuated and uncertainty reduced), classical realists that a multi-polar system is most stable (more sources of deterrence against aggressors). The two theories can be treated as variations within a discourse of realism, so when I refer to realism as a discourse it covers both these positions.

7   For a detailed mapping of environmental discourses and their history, see Dryzek (2005).

8   "Deliberative democracy" and "discursive democracy" are often used synonymously. "Discursive" is actually the better term because interpersonal communication is central to democracy, while deliberation can take place in the solitary human mind. In Dryzek (2000: 3), I recover discursive democracy as a critical approach that resists liberal constitutionalist deliberative democracy's close ties to the formal institutions of existing liberal democratic states, though both "liberal constitutionalist deliberative democracy" and "discursive democracy" fall under the general umbrella of deliberative democracy. Transnational discursive democracy as presented here is consistent with that pluralistic, reflexive, and critical orientation.

9   Civil society can also be home to some very bad things, such as the murderous identity conflicts analyzed in chapter 3. In addition, civil society is sometimes invoked in support of neoliberal market-oriented governance (Chandhoke, 2003; Heins, 2004), which is problematic from the point of view of discursive democracy.

10 Anthony Giddens (1984) speaks of social structures in general in these terms: as both enabling and constraining action, which in turns helps reproduce structures.

Chapter 2   From the Clash of Civilizations to the Engagement of Discourses

1   Gould (2004: 50–74) believes the emergence of norms from engagement across difference is a powerful alternative to moral universalism emanating from the West.

Chapter 3   Deliberation in Divided Societies

1   Putzel (2005: 13) notes that "new wars" are actually similar to the kinds of wars fought before the rise of sovereign states.

2   Democracy is not silent on interstate conflict; the "democratic peace" thesis holds that democratic states never fight one another (Russett and O'Neal, 2001). This thesis in turn provides one prop for neoconservative ideology in the United States, which envisages a more peaceful world once troublesome states (like Saddam Hussein's Iraq) are turned into "democracies." However, the democratic peace thesis has adherents elsewhere on the political spectrum.

3   The recent history of agonism also owes much to Hannah Arendt, William Connolly (1991), and Bonnie Honig (1993).

4   Young (2000: 77–9) proposes a complementary set of standards: to ask if an intervention is "respectful, publicly assertable, and does it stand up to public challenge?"

5   A better approach to electoral democracy in divided societies is the "electoral engineering" proposed by Horowitz (1985) and given flesh by Reilly (2001). Reilly shows that "centripetal" politics can be induced by systems of preferential voting such as the alternative vote (AV), supplementary vote (SV), and single transferable vote (STV). STV combines preferential voting with proportional representation in multi-member constituencies. The ballot requires voters to rank all candidates. Candidates achieving a "quota" are declared elected; their surplus votes are then redistributed, along with the second preferences of candidates eliminated on the basis of their low number of first preferences. If there are (say) six seats per constituency, a quota could be 16.67 percent of votes. AV uses single-member constituencies, again requiring voters to rank all candidates. Candidates are eliminated beginning with those with the fewest first preferences, the votes for eliminated candidates being reallocated according to the next

preference on the ballot. Under SV, voters identify only their first and second preferences for candidates in a single-member constituency. If no candidate receives a majority of first preferences, all but the top two candidates (based on first preferences) are eliminated, and second choices of votes for all the other candidates are reallocated to determine the winner. Leaders of ethnic parties have an incentive to seek second, third, and fourth preferences of voters from the other side of the ethnic divide, and so moderate their positions. Reilly's clearest positive example is Papua New Guinea, which used the Australian-model AV before it foolishly changed to first-past-the-post voting in 1975. If there are not enough voters with moderate attitudes, preferential voting will fail to assist reconciliation – as shown by elections in Northern Ireland in 1973 and 1982 conducted under STV. Only in 1998, after "a core group of moderates emerges from both sides of the communal divide" does STV work better in Northern Ireland (Reilly, 2001: 136–7). This finding begs the question of exactly how moderate attitudes can be promoted. Perhaps AV would work better than STV in Northern Ireland, in keeping with Horowitz's (1991: 189) claim that, though majoritarian, it promotes moderation better precisely because it has a majority threshold. So unlike STV, under AV members cannot be elected with the support only of a hardline minority. However, Reilly shows with reference to the use of AV in Fiji that if the engineering is not done precisely right, instability and violence can still result. Apparently technical aspects of the AV system specified as part of the 1997 Fijian electoral reform turned out to favor ethnic Indian parties, whose success led to an indigeist coup in 2000. Parallel problems have arisen with the use of SV in Sri Lanka. Precision electoral engineering is difficult in the charged setting of a divided society, especially once different sides realize that rules are not neutral, and so try to influence their content. The deadly numbers game is transferred to the meta level. Some kind of preferential voting is clearly best for divided societies. My point is simply that electoral engineering is not enough, because there is so much more to politics than elections.

6 However, some electoral systems are better than others when it comes to promoting discursive engagement in a divided society. Preferential voting (see note 5) has the merits of

promoting communication across divides involving voters as well as leaders.

Chapter 4   Discourses of Error in the War on Terror

1   Oddly, this mistake is shared by Carol Gould's (2004: 261) feminist analysis of terrorism, when she refers to "powerful leaders who undemocratically instruct the foot soldiers what to do" in terrorist operations such as al-Qaeda.

2   The term al-Qaeda is normally translated as "the base." As Burke (2003: 2) points out, the term can also be translated as "precept, rule, principle, maxim, formula or method" or foundation (for a new society), all of which indicate a more discourse-like meaning.

3   This notion of hegemony resembles that articulated in the 1920s by Italian Marxist Antonio Gramsci.

4   Risse (2000) identifies three categories of international action: the logic of strategy associated with rational choice theory, the logic of appropriateness characterizing constructivism, and a logic of arguing based on Habermas's theory of communicative action. Reflexive action represents a fourth type, so we can speak of a "logic of reflexivity."

5   <http://www.gallup-international.com/surveys.htm>. Accessed July 8, 2003.

6   In Australia, the public perception was shared by the Director General of the Australian Security Intelligence Organization, Dennis Richardson: "The fact that we are in close alliance with the US and the fact that we were early and actively engaged in the war on terrorism does contribute to us being a target" (*Canberra Times*, August 13, 2003, p. 1).

Chapter 5   Contesting Globalization

1   Hirst and Thompson point out that the global economy today is perhaps less integrated than it was before World War I, that most of the Third World remains outside the global system, bypassed by flows of trade, investment, and finance.

2   Regimes can also embody regulations, rights, incentive mechanisms, and compliance mechanisms (see Krasner, 1983, for detailed discussions). Examples would include the fisheries regime of the North Atlantic, the global climate regime, the

international trade regime.

3   The international relations discussion has not always been completely satisfactory, inasmuch as "governance" for authors like Rosenau encompasses relatively formalized arrangements such as treaties as well as more informal ones. That is, many international relations scholars have drawn the line in a place that actually includes a lot of the formal authority of "government" under the "governance" heading.

Chapter 6   Reflexivity and Resistance

1   While sustainable development is defined first and foremost in terms of its belief that environmental and economic values can stand in a positive-sum relationship, historically the discourse has also entailed a power shift emphasizing the role of civil society actors in helping to negotiate developmental paths (Dryzek, 2005: ch. 7).

2   I take the title of this section from the slogan of the anti-capitalist May Day 2000 Guerrilla Gardening protestors in London, who dug up Parliament Square.

Chapter 7   Governing Discourses: The Limits of Liberal Multilateralism

1   Multilateralism comes in for a variety of criticisms that I will not address here. It is attacked by market-oriented economists for its facilitation of self-profiting behavior by NGOs and other special interests, by postmodernists and multiculturalists for its repression of cultural diversity, by feminists for the complicity of some international organizations (including peacekeeping operations) in the oppression of women, and by American unilateralists for being under the influence of unaccountable NGOs and international bureaucrats. For a survey of these criticisms, see Alvarez, 2000.

2   Beck's advocacy of stronger international government is also inconsistent with the bulk of his work on the nature of contemporary "risk societies," which is much more attuned to novel and decentralized forms of political organization in response to a variety of risks – nuclear, environmental, and technological.

3   Bohman (2004: 321) defines juridification as "the increasing

expansion of law and law-like methods of formal rules and adjudication to new domains of social life."

4　When such horror stories come from the right of the political spectrum they are usually accompanied by an argument about the superior capacity of market systems to cope with a complex world. For example, Hayek (1979: 65–97) treats the market as a system where actors pursue their interests in circumstances of incomplete and imperfect bits of knowledge held by different and not especially rational persons. What the market does so well is simplify and transmit information in the form of price signals, which enables numerous actors to harmonize what they do without necessarily even being aware of each others' existence. Good individual and collective problem-solving can prosper under such circumstances because it is immediately rewarded in the form of income and profit. Though market enthusiasts have over the past two decades argued that markets are a universal remedy for just about every policy problem, and have convinced policy-makers in many countries of their virtues, experience now demonstrates the many things that a market cannot order, beginning with provision of the legal system and property rights that the market itself needs in order to function. The market of itself provides no protection against mafia capitalism of the Russian variety, cannot defend against corruption, cannot secure social justice, cannot provide public goods such as environmental quality, cannot provide any antidotes to cultural imperialism, cannot fight a war, cannot respond to terrorism.

5　These problems reach beyond a much older conflict between constitutionalism and democracy, which stems from the fact that constitutional specification of rights enables unelected judges to overturn the wishes of electoral majorities.

Chapter 8　Three Kinds of Democracy

1　Among many debates on the pros and cons of the cosmopolitan model, see Holden (1999).

References

Ackerman, Bruce A. 1991. *We the People. I: Foundations*. Cambridge, MA: Harvard University Press.

Alexander, Christopher. 1965. A City is Not a Tree. *Architectural Forum*, 122 (1 and 2): 58–61 and 58–62.

Alvarez, José E. 2000. Multilateralism and its Discontents. *European Journal of International Law*, 11: 393–411.

Anderson, Benedict. 1983. *Imagined Communities: Reflections on the Origin and Spread of Nationalism*. London: Verso.

Andrews, Richard N. L. 1997. United States. In Martin Jänicke and Helmut Weidner, eds., *National Environmental Policies: A Comparative Study of Capacity-Building*. Berlin: Springer, pp. 25–44.

Archibugi, Daniele. 2004. Cosmopolitan Democracy and its Critics. *European Journal of International Relations*, 10: 437–73.

Archibugi, Daniele and David Held, eds. 1995. *Cosmopolitan Democracy: An Agenda for a New World Order*. Cambridge: Polity.

Archibugi, Daniele, David Held, and Martin Köhler, eds. 1998. *Re-Imagining Political Community: Studies in Cosmopolitan Democracy*. Cambridge: Polity.

Bachrach, Peter and Morton S. Baratz. 1962. Two Faces of Power. *American Political Science Review*, 56: 947–52.

Beck, Ulrich. 1992. *Risk Society: Towards a New Modernity*. London: Sage.

Beck, Ulrich. 1999. *What is Globalization?* Cambridge: Polity.

Beck, Ulrich. 2001. The Silence of Words and Political Dynamics in

References

the World Risk Society. Accessed online at <http://logosonline. home.igc.org/beck.htm>.

Beck, Ulrich, Anthony Giddens, and Scott Lash. 1994. *Reflexive Modernization: Politics, Tradition, and Aesthetics in the Modern Social Order*. Cambridge: Polity.

Berejikian, Jeffrey and John S. Dryzek. 2000. Reflexive Action in International Politics. *British Journal of Political Science*, 30: 193–216.

Barber, Benjamin R. 1995. *Jihad vs. McWorld: How Globalism and Tribalism are Reshaping the World*. New York: Ballantine.

Benhabib, Seyla. 1996. Toward a Deliberative Model of Democratic Legitimacy. In Seyla Benhabib, ed., *Democracy and Difference: Contesting the Boundaries of the Political*. Princeton: Princeton University Press, pp. 67–94.

Benhabib, Seyla. 2002. *The Claims of Culture: Equality and Diversity in the Global Era*. Princeton: Princeton University Press.

Bessette, Joseph M. 1994. *The Mild Voice of Reason: Deliberative Democracy and American National Government*. Chicago: University of Chicago Press.

Bohman, James. 2004. Constitution Making and Democratic Innovation: The European Union and Transnational Governance. *European Journal of Political Theory*, 3: 315–37.

Bourdieu, Pierre. 1993. *The Field of Cultural Production*. New York: Columbia University Press.

Bryner, Gary C. 2000. The United States: "Sorry – Not Our Problem." In William M. Lafferty and James Meadowcroft, eds., *Implementing Sustainable Development: Strategies and Initiatives in High Consumption Societies*. Oxford: Oxford University Press, pp. 273–302.

Bull, Hedley. 1977. *The Anarchical Society: A Study of Order in World Politics*. London: Macmillan.

Burgmann, Verity. 2003. *Power, Profit and Protest*. Sydney: Allen and Unwin.

Burke, Jason. 2003. What is al-Qaeda? *The Observer* (London), July 13. Accessed online at <http://observer.guardian.co.uk/world-view/story/0,11581,996509,00.html>.

Burke, Jason. 2004. Think Again: Al-Qaeda. *Foreign Policy*, May/June. Accessed online at <www.foreignpolicy.com/story/cms.php?story_id=2536&print=1>.

Calhoun, Craig. 2002. The Class Consciousness of Frequent Travellers: Towards a Critique of Actually Existing Cosmopolitanism.

References

In Steven Vertovec and Robin Cohen, eds., *Conceiving Cosmopolitanism: Theory, Context, and Practice*. Oxford: Oxford University Press, pp. 86–109.

Castells, Manuel. 1996. *The Information Age, Volume I: The Rise of the Network Society*. Oxford: Basil Blackwell.

Chambers, Simone. 2003. Deliberative Democratic Theory. *Annual Review of Political Science*, 6: 307–26.

Chambers, Simone and Jeffrey Kopstein. 2001. Bad Civil Society. *Political Theory*, 29: 837–65.

Chandhoke, Neera. 2003. *The Conceits of Civil Society*. New Delhi: Oxford University Press.

Checkel, Jeffrey. 1988. The Constructivist Turn in International Relations Theory. *World Politics*, 50: 324–8.

Cochran, Molly. 1999. *Normative Theory in International Relations*. Cambridge: Cambridge University Press.

Cochran, Molly. 2002. A Democratic Critique of Cosmopolitan Democracy: Pragmatism from the Bottom Up. *European Journal of International Relations*, 8: 517–48.

Connolly, William E. 1991. *Identity/Difference: Democratic Negotiations of Political Paradox*. Ithaca, NY: Cornell University Press.

Dahl, Robert A. 1956. *A Preface to Democratic Theory*. Chicago: University of Chicago Press.

Dahl, Robert A. 1963. *Modern Political Analysis*. Englewood Cliffs, NJ: Prentice Hall.

Dalrymple, Rawdon. 1998. Indonesia and the IMF: The Evolving Consequences of a Reforming Mission. *Australian Journal of International Affairs*, 52: 233–9.

Deveaux, Monique. 2003. A Deliberative Approach to Conflicts of Culture. *Political Theory*, 31: 780–807.

Dryzek, John S. 1987a. *Rational Ecology: Environment and Political Economy*. New York: Basil Blackwell.

Dryzek, John S. 1987b. Complexity and Rationality in Public Life. *Political Studies*, 35: 424–42.

Dryzek, John S. 1990. *Discursive Democracy: Politics, Policy, and Political Science*. Cambridge: Cambridge University Press.

Dryzek, John S. 1996. *Democracy in Capitalist Times: Ideals, Limits, and Struggles*. New York: Oxford University Press.

Dryzek, John S. 2000. *Deliberative Democracy and Beyond: Liberals, Critics, Contestations*. Oxford: Oxford University Press.

Dryzek, John S. 2001. Legitimacy and Economy in Deliberative Democracy. *Political Theory*, 29: 651–69.

References

Dryzek, John S. 2004. Constitutionalism and its Alternatives. In Anne van Aaken, Christian List, and Christoph Luetge, eds., *Deliberation and Decision: Economics, Constitutional Theory, and Deliberative Democracy*. Aldershot: Ashgate, pp. 47–59.

Dryzek, John S. 2005. *The Politics of the Earth: Environmental Discourses*. Oxford: Oxford University Press.

Dryzek, John S., David Downes, Christian Hunold, David Schlosberg, with Hans-Kristian Hernes. 2003. *Green States and Social Movements: Environmentalism in the United States, United Kingdom, Germany, and Norway*. Oxford: Oxford University Press.

Fennema, Meindert and Marcel Maussen. 2000. Dealing with Extremists in Political Discussion: Front National and "Front Republicain" in France. *Journal of Political Philosophy* 8: 379–400.

Finnemore, Martha and Kathryn Sikkink. 2001. Taking Stock: The Constructivist Research Program in International Relations and Comparative Politics. *Annual Review of Political Science*, 4: 391–416.

Fish, Stanley. 1999. Mutual Respect as a Device of Exclusion. In Stephen Macedo, ed., *Deliberative Politics: Essays on Democracy and Disagreement*. New York: Oxford University Press, pp. 88–102.

Fishkin, James. 1995. *The Voice of the People: Public Opinion and Democracy*. New Haven, CT: Yale University Press.

Forester, John. 1999a. *The Deliberative Practitioner*. Cambridge, MA: MIT Press.

Forester, John. 1999b. Dealing with Deep Value Differences. In Lawrence Susskind, ed., *The Consensus Building Handbook*. Thousand Oaks, CA: Sage, pp. 463–93.

Foucault, Michel. 1980. *Power/Knowledge*. Brighton: Harvester.

Frey, Bruno S. 1988. Fighting Political Terrorism by Refusing Recognition. *Journal of Public Policy*, 7: 179–88.

Frey, Bruno S. and Simon Luechinger. 2004. Decentralisation as a Disincentive to Terror. *European Journal of Political Economy*, 20: 590–615.

Frynas, J. George. 2003. Global Monitor: Royal Dutch/Shell. *New Political Economy*, 8: 275–85.

Fukuyama, Francis. 1989. The End of History? *National Interest* (Summer): 3–18.

Fukuyama, Francis. 1992. *The End of History and the Last Man*. New York: Free Press.

References

Gambetta, Diego. 2004. Reason and Terror: Has 9/11 Made it Hard to Think Straight? *Boston Review*. Accessed online at <http://bostonreview.net/BR29.2/gambetta.html>.

George, Jim. 1994. *Discourses of Global Politics: A Critical (Re)Introduction to International Relations*. Boulder, CO: Lynne Rienner.

Giddens, Anthony. 1984. *The Constitution of Society: Outline of the Theory of Structuration*. Berkeley: University of California Press.

Giddens, Anthony. 1998. *The Third Way*. Cambridge: Polity.

Giddens, Anthony. 2000. *Runaway World: How Globalization is Reshaping our Lives*. London: Routledge and Kegan Paul.

Gould, Carol C. 2004. *Globalizing Democracy and Human Rights*. Cambridge: Cambridge University Press.

Gutmann, Amy and Dennis Thompson. 1996. *Democracy and Disagreement*. Cambridge, MA: Harvard University Press.

Habermas, Jürgen. 1984. *The Theory of Communicative Action I: Reason and the Rationalization of Society*. Boston: Beacon Press.

Habermas, Jürgen. 1996. *Between Facts and Norms: Contributions to a Discourse Theory of Law and Democracy*. Cambridge, MA: MIT Press.

Habermas, Jürgen. 2001. *The Postnational Constellation*. Cambridge, MA: MIT Press.

Hajer, Maarten A. 1993. Discourse Coalitions and the Institutionalization of Practice: The Case of Acid Rain in Great Britain. In Frank Fischer and John Forester, eds., *The Argumentative Turn in Policy Analysis and Planning*. Durham, NC: Duke University Press, pp. 43–76.

Hajer, Maarten A. 2003. Policy without Polity? Policy Analysis and the Institutional Void. *Policy Sciences* 36: 175–95.

Hajer, Maarten A. and Hendrik Wagenaar, eds., 2003. *Deliberative Policy Analysis: Understanding Governance in the Network Society*. Cambridge: Cambridge University Press.

Hall, Rodney Bruce. 2003. The Discursive Demolition of the Asian Development Model. *International Studies Quarterly*, 47: 71–99.

Hathaway, James C. 2000. America, Defender of Democratic Legitimacy? *European Journal of International Law*, 11: 121–34.

Hay, Colin. 1998. Globalization, Welfare Retrenchment, and the Logic of No Alternative. *Journal of Social Policy*, 27: 525–32.

Hay, Colin and Ben Rosamond. 2002. Globalisation, European Integration, and the Discursive Construction of Economic Imperatives. *Journal of European Public Policy*, 9: 147–67.

Hayek, Friedrich A. von. 1979. *Law, Legislation, and Liberty: The*

References

Political Order of a Free People. Chicago: University of Chicago Press.

Heins, Volker. 2004. Civil Society's Barbarisms. *European Journal of Social Theory*, 7: 499–517.

Held, David. 1995. *Democracy and the Global Order: From the Nation-state to Cosmopolitan Governance*. Cambridge: Polity.

Held, David. 2003. Return to the State of Nature. *Open Democracy*, 3/20/2003. Accessed online at <www.opendemocracy.net/debates/article–2–88–1065.jsp>, April 21, 2004.

Held, David. 2004. *Global Covenant: The Social Democratic Alternative to the Washington Consensus*. Cambridge: Polity.

Held, David and Anthony McGrew. 2000. The Great Globalization Debate: An Introduction. In David Held and Anthony McGrew, eds., *The Global Transformations Reader*. Cambridge: Polity, pp. 1–45.

Higgott, Richard. 2004. Multilateralism and the Limits of Global Governance. Working paper no. 134/04, Centre for the Study of Globalization and Regionalization, University of Warwick, UK.

Hirst, Paul and Grahame Thompson. 1996. *Globalization in Question: The International Economy and the Possibilities of Governance*. Cambridge: Polity.

Holden, Barry, ed. 1999. *Global Democracy: Key Debates*. London: Routledge.

Honig, Bonnie. 1993. *Political Theory and the Displacement of Politics*. Ithaca, NY: Cornell University Press.

Horowitz, Donald. 1985. *Ethnic Groups in Conflict*. Berkeley: University of California Press.

Horowitz, Donald. 1991. *A Democratic South Africa? Constitutional Engineering in a Divided Society*. Berkeley: University of California Press.

Horowitz, Donald. 2000. Constitutional Design: An Oxymoron? In Ian Shapiro and Stephen Macedo, eds., *Designing Democratic Institutions (Nomos XLII)*. New York: New York University Press, pp. 253–84.

Huntington, Samuel P. 1993. The Clash of Civilizations. *Foreign Affairs*, 72(3): 22–49.

Huntington, Samuel P. 1996. *The Clash of Civilizations and the Remaking of World Order*. New York: Simon and Schuster.

Huntington, Samuel P. 2004. *Who Are We? The Challenges to America's National Identity*. New York: Simon and Schuster.

References

Ikenberry, G. John. 2001. *After Victory: Institutions, Strategic Restraint, and the Rebuilding of Order After Major Wars*. Princeton: Princeton University Press.

Kaldor, Mary. 1999. *New and Old Wars: Organized Violence in a Global Era*. Cambridge: Polity.

Kaldor, Mary. 2003. *Global Civil Society: An Answer to War*. Cambridge: Polity.

Kanra, Bora. 2005. Deliberation Across Difference: Bringing Social Learning Into the Theory and Practice of Deliberative Democracy in the Case of Turkey. Unpublished PhD thesis, Research School of Social Sciences, Australian National University.

Kapoor, Ilan. 2002. Deliberative Democracy or Agonistic Pluralism? The Relevance of the Habermas–Mouffe Debate for Third World Politics. *Alternatives*, 27: 459–87.

Kaufman, Stuart J. 2001. *Modern Hatreds: The Symbolic Politics of Ethnic War*. Ithaca, NY: Cornell University Press.

Keal, Paul. 2000. An "International Society"? In Greg Fry and Jacinta O'Hagan, eds., *Contending Images of World Politics*. Houndmills: Macmillan, pp. 61–75.

Keene, Edward. 2002. *Beyond the Anarchical Society: Grotius, Colonialism and Order in World Politics*. Cambridge: Cambridge University Press.

Kendal, Gavin. 1997. "Governing at a Distance": Anglo-Australian Relations, 1840–1870. *Australian Journal of Political Science*, 32: 223–36.

Kersch, Ken. 2004. Multilateralism Comes to the Courts. *The Public Interest*, 154 (Winter).

Kissinger, Henry. 2001. America at the Apex. *The National Interest* (Summer).

Krasner, Stephen D. 1983. Structural Causes and Regime Consequences: Regimes as Intervening Variables. In Stephen D. Krasner, ed., *International Regimes*. Ithaca, NY: Cornell University Press, pp. 1–21.

Krasner, Stephen D. 1999. *Sovereignty: Organized Hypocrisy*. Princeton: Princeton University Press.

Kymlicka, Will. 1995. *Multicultural Citizenship*. Oxford: Oxford University Press.

Lafferty, William M. 1996. The Politics of Sustainable Development. *Environmental Politics*, 5 (2): 185–208.

Lieven, Anatol. 2004a. Demon in the Cellar. *Prospect*, 96 (March): 28–33.

References

Lieven, Anatol. 2004b. *America Right or Wrong: An Anatomy of American Nationalism*. New York: HarperCollins.

Lijphart, Arend. 1977. *Democracy in Plural Societies: A Comparative Exploration*. New Haven, CT: Yale University Press.

Lijphart, Arend. 1994. Prospects for Power Sharing in the New South Africa. In Andrew Reynolds, ed., *Election '94 South Africa: An Analysis of the Results, Campaign and Future Prospects*. New York: St Martin's.

Lijphart, Arend. 2000. Varieties of Nonmajoritarian Democracy. In Markus M. L. Crepaz, Thomas A. Koelble, and David Wilsford, eds., *Democracy and Institutions: The Life Work of Arend Lijphart*. Ann Arbor: University of Michigan Press, pp. 225–46.

Lindblom, Charles E. 1982. The Market as Prison. *Journal of Politics*, 44: 324–36.

Litfin, Karen T. 1994. *Ozone Discourses: Science and Politics in Global Environmental Cooperation*. New York: Columbia University Press.

Lomborg, Bjørn. 2001. *The Skeptical Environmentalist: Measuring the Real State of the World*. Cambridge: Cambridge University Press.

Lukes, Steven. 1974. *Power: A Radical View*. London: Macmillan.

Mackie, Gerry. 1996. Ending Footbinding and Infibulation: A Convention Account. *American Sociological Review*, 61: 999–1017.

Mackie, Gerry. 2002. Does Democratic Deliberation Change Minds? Paper presented at the Annual Meeting of the American Political Science Association, Boston.

McGrew, Anthony. 2002. Transnational Democracy. In April Carter and Geoffrey Stokes, eds., *Democratic Theory Today*. Cambridge: Polity, pp. 269–94.

Marsh, David and Nicola Jo-Anne Smith. 2004. Globalisation, the Discourse of Globalisation and the Hollowing Out of the State. Unpublished paper, University of Birmingham.

Meadows, Donella H., Dennis L. Meadows, Jørgen Randers, and William H. Behrens III. 1972. *The Limits to Growth*. New York: Universe Books.

Milliken, Jennifer. 1999. The Study of Discourse in International Relations: A Critique of Research and Methods. *European Journal of International Relations*, 5: 225–54.

Moore, Margaret. 1999. Beyond the Cultural Argument for Liberal Nationalism. *Critical Review of International Social and Political Philosophy*, 2: 26–47.

References

Morgenthau, Hans. 1985. *Politics Among Nations: The Struggle for Power and Peace*. New York: Knopf.

Mouffe, Chantal. 1999. Deliberative Democracy or Agonistic Pluralism? *Social Research*, 66: 745–58.

Mouffe, Chantal. 2000a. *The Democratic Paradox*. London: Verso.

Mouffe, Chantal. 2000b. Deliberative Democracy or Agonistic Pluralism? Vienna: Institute for Advanced Studies, Political Science Series, No. 72.

Neumann, Iver B. 2002. Returning Practice to the Linguistic Turn: The Case of Diplomacy. *Millennium*, 31: 627–51.

Nye, Joseph S., Jr. 2002. *The Paradox of American Power: Why the World's Only Superpower Cannot Go It Alone*. New York: Oxford University Press.

Nye, Joseph S., Jr. 2003. Propaganda Isn't the Way: Soft Power. *International Herald Tribune*, January 10. Accessed online at <www.ksg.harvard.edu/news/opeds/2003/nye_soft-power_iht_011003.htm>.

Nye, Joseph S., Jr. 2004. *Soft Power: The Means to Success in World Politics*. New York: Public Affairs.

Offe, Claus. 2001. *Security in a Time of Hatred*. Berlin: Humboldt University.

O'Hagan, Jacinta. 2000. A "Clash of Civilizations"? In Greg Fry and Jacinta O'Hagan, eds., *Contending Images of World Politics*. Houndmills: Macmillan, pp. 135–49.

Orbell, John M., Alphons J. C. van de Kragt, and Robyn M. Dawes. 1988. Explaining Discussion-Induced Cooperation in Social Dilemmas. *Journal of Personality and Social Psychology*, 54: 811–19.

Patomäki, Heikki. 2003. Problems of Democratizing Global Governance: Time, Space and the Emancipatory Process. *European Journal of International Relations*, 9: 347–76.

Popper, Karl R. 1966. *The Open Society and its Enemies*. London: Routledge and Kegan Paul.

Prestowitz, Clyde. 2003. *Rogue Nation: American Unilateralism and the Failure of Good Intentions*. New York: Basic Books.

Price, Richard and Christian Reus-Smit. 1998. Dangerous Liaisons? Critical International Theory and Constructivism. *European Journal of International Relations*, 4: 259–94.

Putzel, James. 2005. Globalization, Liberalization, and the Prospects for the State. *International Political Science Review*, 26: 5–16.

References

Rae, Heather. 2002. *State Identities and the Homogenisation of Peoples*. Cambridge: Cambridge University Press.

Rawls, John. 1993. *Political Liberalism*. New York: Columbia University Press.

Rawls, John. 1997. The Idea of Public Reason Revisited. *University of Chicago Law Review*, 94: 765–807.

Reilly, Benjamin. 2001. *Democracy in Divided Societies: Electoral Engineering for Conflict Management*. Cambridge: Cambridge University Press.

Reus-Smit, Christian. 1999. *The Moral Purpose of the State: Culture, Social Identity, and Institutional Rationality in International Relations*. Princeton: Princeton University Press.

Reus-Smit, Christian. 2004. *American Power and World Order*. Cambridge: Polity.

Reynolds, Andrew. 2000. Majoritarian or Power-Sharing Government. In Markus M. L. Crepaz, Thomas A. Koelble, and David Wilsford, eds., *Democracy and Institutions: The Life Work of Arend Lijphart*. Ann Arbor: University of Michigan Press, pp. 155–96.

Risse, Thomas. 2000. "Let's Argue!" Communicative Action in World Politics. *International Organization*, 54: 1–39.

Rose, Chris. 1998. *The Turning of the Spar*. London: Greenpeace.

Rosenau, James N. 1992. Governance, Order, and Change in World Politics. In James N. Rosenau and Ernst-Otto Czempiel, eds., *Governance Without Government: Order and Change in World Politics*. New York: Cambridge University Press, pp. 1–29.

Rosenau, James N. 1998. Governance and Democracy in a Globalizing World. In Daniele Archibugi, David Held, and Martin Köhler, eds., *Re-Imagining Political Community: Studies in Cosmopolitan Democracy*. Cambridge: Polity, pp. 28–57.

Rosenau, James N. and Ernst-Otto Czempiel, eds. 1992. *Governance Without Government: Order and Change in World Politics*. New York: Cambridge University Press.

Rueschemeyer, Dietrich, Evelyn Huber Stevens, and John D. Stevens. 1992. *Capitalist Development and Democracy*. Chicago: University of Chicago Press.

Ruggie, John G. 1982. International Regimes, Transactions and Change: Embedded Liberalism in the Postwar Economic Order. *International Organization*, 35: 379–415.

Ruggie, John G., ed. 1993. *Multilateralism Matters: The Theory and Praxis of an Institutional Form*. New York: Columbia University Press.

182

References

Ruggie, John G. 1998. What Makes the World Hang Together? Neo-Utilitarianism and the Social Constructivist Challenge. *International Organization*, 52: 855–87.

Russett, Bruce and John Oneal. 2001. *Triangulating Peace: Democracy, Interdependence, and International Organizations*. New York: W. W. Norton.

Scheuerman, William E. 2006. Critical Theory Beyond Habermas. In John S. Dryzek, Bonnie Honig, and Anne Phillips, eds., *The Oxford Handbook of Political Theory*. Oxford: Oxford University Press.

Schlosberg, David. 1999. *Environmental Justice and the New Pluralism: The Challenge of Difference for Environmentalism*. Oxford: Oxford University Press, pp. 85–105.

Scott, James C. 1998. *Seeing Like a State: How Certain Schemes to Improve the Human Condition Have Failed*. New Haven, CT: Yale University Press.

Simon, Herbert A. 1981. *The Sciences of the Artificial*, 2nd edn Cambridge, MA: MIT Press, pp. 85–105.

Simon, William H. 1999. Three Limitations of Deliberative Democracy: Identity Politics, Bad Faith, and Indeterminacy. In Stephen Macedo, ed., *Deliberative Politics: Essays on Democracy and Disagreement*. New York: Oxford University Press, pp. 49–57.

Slaughter, Anne-Marie. 1997. The Real New World Order. *Foreign Affairs*, 76 (5): 183–97.

Slaughter, Anne-Marie. 2004. We Can Beat Terror at its Own Game: Networks as Both the Problem and the Solution. *Los Angeles Times*, April 25. Accessed online at <www.latimes. com/news/printededition/opinion/la-op-slaughter>.

Snyder, Jack and Karen Ballentine. 1996. Nationalism and the Marketplace of Ideas. *International Security*, 21: 5–40.

Stiglitz, Joseph. 2002. *Globalization and its Discontents*. New York: W. W. Norton.

Sunstein, Cass R. 2002. The Law of Group Polarization. *Journal of Political Philosophy*, 10: 175–95.

Teschke, Benno. 1997. Geopolitical Relations in the European Middle Ages: History and Theory. *International Organization*, 52: 325–58.

Thompson, Dennis. 1999. Democratic Theory and Global Society. *Journal of Political Philosophy*, 7: 111–25.

Torgerson, Douglas. 1995. The Uncertain Quest for Sustainability: Public Discourse and the Politics of Environmentalism. In Frank

References

Fischer and Michael Black, eds., *Greening Environmental Policy: The Politics of a Sustainable Future*. Liverpool: Paul Chapman, pp. 3–20.

Tribe, Laurence. 1973. Technology Assessment and the Fourth Discontinuity: The Limits of Instrumental Rationality. *Southern California Law Review*, 46: 617–60.

Truman, David B. 1951. *The Governmental Process*. New York: Knopf.

US Department of State. 2003. *Patterns of Global Terrorism*. Washington, DC: US Department of State.

van Ham, Peter. 2002. Branding Territory: Inside the Wonderful Worlds of PR and IR Theory. *Millennium*, 31: 249–69.

Varese, Federico. 2001. *The Russian Mafia*. Oxford: Oxford University Press.

Walker, R. B. J. 1993. *Inside/Outside: International Relations as Political Theory*. Cambridge: Cambridge University Press.

Waltz, Kenneth N. 1979. *Theory of International Politics*. Reading: Addison-Wesley.

Walzer, Michael. 1996. Spheres of Affection. In Martha Nussbaum, ed., *For Love of Country: Debating the Limits of Patriotism*. Boston: Beacon Press.

Weldes, Jutta and Diana Saco. 1996. Making State Action Possible: The United States and the Discursive Construction of "the Cuban Problem." *Millennium*, 25: 361–95.

Wendt, Alexander. 1992. Anarchy is What States Make of It: The Social Construction of Power Politics. *International Organization*, 46: 391–425.

Wendt, Alexander. 1999. *Social Theory of International Politics*. Cambridge: Cambridge University Press.

Wolf, Martin. 2004. *Why Globalization Works*. New Haven, CT: Yale University Press.

Young, Iris Marion. 1997. Difference as a Resource for Democratic Communication. In James Bohman and William Rehg, eds., *Deliberative Democracy*. Cambridge: MIT Press, pp. 383–406.

Young, Iris Marion. 2000. *Inclusion and Democracy*. Oxford: Oxford University Press.

Young, Oran R. 1994. *International Governance: Protecting the Environment in a Stateless Society*. Ithaca, NY: Cornell University Press.

Index

Index

Index

Rawls, John 47
Reagan, Ronald 18
realism 2, 8, 11–13, 31, 92, 114, 120, 163, 167n6
reasoning
  constitutive 113–17
  instrumental 113–14
reflexive action ix, 84–6, 89, 110, 111–24, 126–7, 151
reflexive modernization 20–1, 111, 117–19, 126, 143–4, 157
reflexive traditionalization 20–1, 30, 41, 119
regimes 130–1, 170–1n2
Reilly, Benjamin 168n5
relationships, natural 165–6n1
representation, group 56
resistance ix, 112, 124–5
Reus-Smit, Christian 7, 77, 132, 166n4
Reynolds, Andrew 51
rhetoric 63–4, 166n1
Richardson, Dennis 170n6
risk society 171n2
risks 118–19
Risse, Thomas 26, 170n4
Robertson, George 131
Roosevelt, Theodore 81
Rosenau, James N. 106, 157
rule of law 136
Rumsfeld, Donald 14
Russia 34, 138–9
Rwanda 59, 63

Schlosberg, David 58
Scott, James C. 142
Seattle 10
security 11–14, 83
September 11 (2001) viii, 14, 18, 29, 69, 77, 129, 131, 142, 152

Shell Corporation 99–100, 116, 122
Siro-Wiwa, Ken 100
Slaughter, Anne-Marie 72, 106
Snyder, Jack 59, 60
social democracy 152
social learning 27–8
social movements 63
Soros, George 59
South Africa 65–6
sovereignty 7, 15, 43, 55, 61, 66, 99, 166n4
Soviet Union 115
Sri Lanka 169n5
state
  coercive 139
state-building 33, 55, 57
states 3, 4, 98, 109, 122–3, 162
Stiglitz, Joseph 10, 124, 125
strategic action 4–6
structural adjustment 102
Sunstein, Cass 51, 59
sustainable development 2, 17–18, 82–3, 104, 117, 171n1

technocracy 143
terrorism 16, 86, 87–8, 93, 131, 170n1
Thatcher, Margaret 78
Thompson, Dennis 24, 47
Thompson, Grahame 10, 97, 170n1
Thomson, James 75
trade-related intellectual property rights (TRIPS) 107
Tribe, Laurence 113
Truman, David B. 159
Turkey 40–1, 53–4
Tutu, Desmond 65

190

Index

unilateralism
US 132, 133, 146, 152, 154
United Nations 31, 92, 134
Universal Declaration of
Human Rights 14–15
US domestic politics 81
US Information Agency 78

Walker, R. B. J. 25
Waltz, Kenneth N. 11, 167n6
Walzer, Michael 158
war of ideas 70, 73–7, 82, 85,
91, 93, 94, 111, 153
war on terror viii, 13–14, 69,
73, 75, 76, 86, 119, 134
wars
fault line 31
new 45–6, 168n1
old 47
Washington Consensus 8–9, 79,
97, 102, 124, 159

weapons of mass destruction
134
Weber, Max 125, 141
Wendt, Alexander 11, 12, 25,
115
West, the 30, 89–90
Westphalia, Treaty of 15, 43, 55
Wolf, Martin 96, 109
World Bank 97, 102, 105
World Summit on Sustainable
Development 83, 146
World Trade Organization 83,
98–9, 103, 105, 135, 142
World War II 130

Yew, Lee Kwan 15, 37
Young, Iris Marion 124, 168n4
Young, Oran R. 106
Yugoslavia 35, 46, 53, 67–8

Zapatistas 60